without a map

a journey through grief

suzanne antisdel

COMTEQ
PUBLISHING
MARGATE, NEW JERSEY

Copyright © December 2010 by Suzanne Antisdel

All rights reserved. No part of this book may be used or reproduced in any manner, electronic or mechanical, including photocopying, recording or by any information storage and retrieval system, or otherwise, without written permission from the publisher.

Published by:
    ComteQ Publishing
    A division of ComteQ Communications, LLC
    101 N. Washington Ave. • Suite 2B
    Margate, New Jersey 08402
    609-487-9000 • Fax 609-487-9099
    Email: publisher@ComteQpublishing.com
    Website: www.ComteQpublishing.com

ISBN 978-1-935232-34-6

Cover design by Rob Huberman
Book design by Jackie Caplan & Rob Huberman
Back cover photo by Frank Hammer

Printed in the United States of America
10 9 8 7 6 5 4 3 2 1

Family are friends
Friends are family

Thanks to each one of you for
        egging
        cajoling
        sweettalking
me on to finish this book.
It's yours as much as mine.

CONTENTS

       sudden death 1
       task 2

PREFACE 3

THE AVALANCHE

  loneliness
      maelstrom 7
      perspective 8
      reaching back 9
      scold 10
      numbers 11
      silence 12
      words 13
      laundry 14
      fantasy 15
      suzart 16
      Vesuvius 17
      only one 18
      emptiness 19
      watching 20
      Mario's 21
      anyone? 26

  who we were
      yin yang 29
      for Thor 33

missing him
    changes 36
    parts of speech 37
    impression 38
    we had it all 39
    old habits 41
    equilibrium 42
    bed 43
    shoeshine I 44
    shoeshine II 45
    doing without 46
    not 47
    afternoons 48

THE FOG

things
    milestone 51
    memento 52
    fixing 53
    furnishing 54
    mailbox 55
    house past tense 56
    the attic 57
    clothes 58
    the closet 59
    to the new owners 61

holidays
    plans for hanging on 64
    avalanche 65
    holidays 66
    anniversary 67

regrets
    reassurance 71
    freedom 72
    doubt 73

music
    essence 75
    good jazz 76
    lyrics 77

time
    time out 81
    no date 82

pets
    barca 84
    lax training 87
    putting the dog down 88
    dog gone 89
    leaving 90

self-Image
    cordoned off 92
    commonalities 93
    change the view 94
    movement 95
    now I can…maybe 96
    progress 97

travel
    not yet 102
    coming back to Stratford 107
    Stratford redux 1 108

COPING

coping with depression
gifts 113
sunfire 115
sit this one out 116
the game 117
diversions 118
accumulation 119
crack 120
new vista 121
first dinner party 127
echo 130

support
bed and bereavement 133
support 134
Janice 135
bitter mood 139
good intentions 141

drugs
getaways 143
time extension 144

writing 146

respect 147

THE EXPERIENCES OF OTHERS
Ellie Tudor 150
Lavanya Krishnan 151
Leslie Zillman 151
Jackie Krueger 155
Mary Asscl 157
Marti Alston 159

CONCLUSION 161

sudden death

if we'd had more time to plan
you would have left me
with
good instructions about
which pepper or olive oil
to use
how to drain the furnace
or clean the fish tank filter
or do without you in bed

task

coming home
from the hospital
that night
I saw
the humidifier
soaking in
vinegar
it took a few minutes
to scrub it
finish the job

hours before
you had
been ripped
out of my life
and I was still
bleeding
raw
my guts hanging
from my sides
I didn't notice

PREFACE

On January 18, 2003, my daughter Anne and I stood in the parking lot of Henry Ford Hospital in the freezing Michigan cold, held each other, and wept.

My husband of thirty years had died at 71, following heart surgery. He had fought for thirty hours while we watched at his hospital bedside. When I was told that there was no hope, I gave the approval to turn off all the life support.

I had been in phone contact with my son Jim, a geriatrician in Baltimore, throughout the horrible week end, and he and Anne kept me together. I finally called him to tell him the worst news and I cried, "We never had time to say goodbye!" "You've been saying goodbye for thirty years," was his reply.

Anne and I saw Art's daughters, Lynn and Amy, off to Ann Arbor and left the hospital in a fog. As I was walking out of his room, one of the dear nurses asked if there was anything she could do for me. "Yes," I answered. "You can bring my husband back."

At the time, I had absolutely no idea of what had happened or what was in store for me. And full understanding of that loss didn't come until almost two years later, having gone through the most difficult, the worst period in my life. After about a year, I was calling it an education, when I was feeling good. Mostly I didn't know what to call it and couldn't even come to a point of analyzing my feelings or the process of my grief. What I could do was to write poetry of my feelings, from depression to disorientation to rage. I wrote and wrote and wrote, and I dated what I wrote, knowing that some day I would need to know when I was feeling those feelings.

I have always valued the writing of journals, as a means toward understanding myself. So my journals of grief served two important purposes: to pour out my heart on paper and to chart my progress.

Rereading them later, I lived again through the pain, but I could also say, "Oh! How far I've come!" or at least, "I've moved from that place," or "I'd forgotten how hard it was."

One thing is certain: everyone grieves in her/his own way, and deserves respect and time to do so. Culture, experience, personality, lifestyle, class, race, ethnic background—they all play a part in how we grieve. But through all this runs the common thread of humanity around the globe: we have suffered the loss of a beloved, and the loss, for some of us, has brought on tumultuous changes in our lives.

It is my hope that some of the things I felt and did may be in some way useful to others. Perhaps this book will be to the reader the book I wished I'd had at the time—a look into the diaries of someone else in a similar situation, to find comfort, hope and a few ways to cope. Perhaps you will find in these pages some measure of help in the journey of grief. In my own grief, I never found my map, but it emerged only later as I charted my progress through my writing.

The poems could stand alone as a chronicle of my grief. I began writing them in earnest after the memorial service. Planning every detail of that service helped to keep me going for those first weeks. In the letdown following it, I began to write poetry, trying every metaphor I could think of to express the anguish and pain and confusion I felt. Some are little anecdotes. Some are feelings that were brimming over and had no other place to go but onto paper.

The journals help to fill in with stories that the poems leave out, bringing another perspective to my process. Some of the sections that follow will strike chords with readers. Some will have no relevance at all and may be skipped. Some will possibly be of interest in a year or two. So maybe you'll want to keep the book: if you lend it out to a friend who is going through some hard times, put your name in it.

THE AVALANCHE

loneliness

maelstrom

the house has
come down
swirling around me
during the monsoon
upended
and shaking its
contents into
the swirling
winds

food out of the
refrigerator
flotsam from
kitchen junk drawers
little nails and screws
out of
the basement
pieces of jigsaw puzzles
torn from
carefully tied boxes
in the attic

later
settling into
one gigantic
blurry
mountain of mess

I stand in the echoing field
with
no arms
to put things right again

August 03

perspective

I can see now that
I have a past
and a present
where there was nothing
but void

I know that because
my fingernails are now
long enough
to pick up the cards
after I lose a
game of solitaire

May 03

reaching back

sometimes
with swift suddenness
like the zapping
strike of
grief
comes a brief
dazzling dream

the nightmare
is over
the dark hell
of the past months
never happened
I no longer speak of
　you
in the past tense
or use the single
voice
and we are
us
again

July 03

scold

if you hadn't
died
I
wouldn't have to
do all this stuff to
keep sane
yoga
and naps
and
finding friends
to eat with

August 03

numbers

I've had tea
with the neighbors
at 4
cocktail at 5
9 games of solitaire
waiting for 8
when a movie I'm
bored with
comes on

October 03

silence

in the cavernous house
the phone rings
occasionally

voices
and music
drift in on
airwaves

the din of
memories
and longing
pervades
the silence

November 03

words

"after Art died"
I say the words
but they have no meaning
coming in the
middle of a sentence
a parenthetical phrase
to mark some
other date
before or after

the only one
I know for sure
when something terrible
happened

October 03

laundry

I saw your blood
on the towel you used
—it wouldn't wash away—
one of the last
physical
things I have of you

how easy it would be
if I could
launder out
the memories
and with them
the pain

December 03

fantasy

a fantasy keeps
playing out:
in the midst of friends
glowing with
happiness again
I am announcing
excitedly
Art's coming back!
he's coming back!

the scene stops there
I can't think how
they would reply
but it feels
glorious to say it

May 04

What a terrible loss! I'll always remember the meetings with Ike and our group at your lovely home. Art cooked up wonderful meals for us, and there was always his beautiful smile for all of his friends and colleagues.

Shalom
Bobbi Graff

(Bobbi was Art's colleague and fellow activist.)

suzart

you have encircled me
you encircle me now
you are not
    were not
        there
            but here
I could not tell where
I left off and
you began
you were my aura
I carried you with me

even in dreams
    where I rarely saw you
you were part of
the scene

how do paraplegics
with their guts missing
make it?

May 04

"I miss you already. You are a part of me now, and I feel the loss."
                note I found on returning from a trip

Vesuvius

for so long
so long
the lava of
pain
bubbling up
hot and calamitous
and inexorable
covered the
memories
covered the joy
or the warmth
of recall
pinching your cheeks
biting your ear

choice was not
available
the volcano had
erupted
before I knew it

September 04

Art touched the lives of many people as a man who was actively and humanistically involved in the issues of his time. No more can be asked of any man.

I hope you will find comfort in your memories of your years together, sharing mutual interests and laughter and joys.
Norma Barth

(Norma and her husband Bernie were fellow lefties and strong Detroit activists. Both are now deceased.)

only one

I was never meant to
be without you

from the moment
we met
you began to
worm your way inside me
until I couldn't tell
me
from you

this is a strange
unwanted body
that I have
no desire to
inhabit now

with whatever
being left to me
I resist
but
I am a
weakened warrior
unable to
cope with what
is inevitable

September 04

…You were two halves of a whole and your happiness together was and is an inspiration to us

Karen and David Claire

(Barbara Killinger's son and daughter-in-law)

emptiness

the blank page
nothing

now spring is here
I am still in winter

three months now
meaning nothing

April 03

watching

I see them
together
across the street

it must be nice
to talk
to your husband
in the driveway
about the garden

May 04

Mario's

mangia, mangia
the waiter urges
(it is the first time she
has eaten out
alone)

I remember my mom
she was like this
alone
in pain
so sad without
my dad
I couldn't help her
I felt so sorry
but I couldn't help her

mangia
it will do you good
to eat—
lots of pasta
lots of cheese
comfort food
can I get you something else?

June 03

February 23

Things are quieted down - only a few phone calls, only a few cards. My first time at a public gathering, at Helen's – I didn't know if I'd get through it without tears, and then resented that so few people there talked about me, and Art. How can you all just sit there and discuss news events when I've just been through this earthquake? Don't you miss him? Why don't you say something about it?

Breakdown and tears all the way home in the car. Disappointed that no one invited me to go to dinner with them; disappointed that some close friends are not coming to the memorial. Feeling sorry for myself. Frightened about what I'll do when Joan leaves after the memorial. Disappointed that she's staying only 3 nights with me.

February 25, 2003

Today I crumbled. Stumbled and crumbled.

I woke at 7:30 – a good night's sleep after going to bed around 11:30—maybe that's one of the answers, to stay up—oh, well.

I had some energy and decided to pay some bills. Alexandra called and invited me to have lunch with her on Monday—told her the kids would be here. Then called her back and said no, kids would have gone home, but Joan would be here, so we should all go out together. Three widows. Oh, god.

I laminated Janice's Celtic sympathy poem, made breakfast, and Kim came to pick up the fish water to take for testing. We said we'd see each other on Monday night to go to the Lysistrata Project together.

Then it becomes a blur. Somehow I was crying and trying to call Helen Samberg, who had said to call her even if it was just to cry on the phone. But before I could get through, I dropped the phone and dropped the plastic calendar, both of which separated into clattering, earshattering pieces on the tile floor. I looked at them and slumped to the floor, sobbing. I couldn't call Janice – she's leaving town and has so much to do – so I called Pamm Linton [a neighbor]. She said she was just getting out of the shower and would be right down.

Bless her. She came, hair still wet, and held me. I wanted to go back and sit on the floor in the library where I had first slumped down, so she sat on the couch there and stroked my arm while I sobbed. We talked about everything that was on my mind. She told me of her own grief of losing her mother, a brother and someone else all within a few months. She knew, but I knew she didn't really know, until she has lost Keith. I hope I can be there for her when that happens. Or I hope she has someone as good and helpful there.

After a while I was able to get up, and she made tea, cleaning up the kitchen as she went. She offered, and I took her up on it, to take the memorial program to the printer. She came with me to the computer while I finished what I had to do on it, took my instructions like a perfect secretary, hugged me, and left, taking my outgoing mail.

The new bed we'd ordered [months before] came in the afternoon. I had them put it in the furnace room. Some day I'll put it together in the bedroom but not now, not now. I don't want any changes. I haven't taken T's pajamas down from the hook in the bathroom. I haven't unpacked his clothes from the hospital. I sleep on my side of the bed and haven't moved the pillow he used the night before he left for the hospital.

I keep seeing "death of a spouse" as the first item on the list of Stress-Producing Life Events. The first item. How interesting. Why are human beings so tightly linked when they couple, as we did, so that the wrenching away by death is so wrenching? Anne says she feels raw. I feel as if someone, something has torn my guts, my right arm and leg off me and left me alone to go through life, go through a day as if nothing has happened. Pet the dog, talk on the phone, say, "Fine" when people ask how I am, or "….okay." I don't say fine except to strangers who don't know what's going on.

Nights were the worst, but some days were unbearable. I had lost any resources to deal with the slightest problem and this was an overwhelming one. It was at night that I would give in to screaming. At night, when I was getting ready for bed, my energy at its lowest ebb, my screams would resound along the tile walls of my bathroom. I think I screamed, "I can't! I can't DO this!" It was my letting-go, and I sank exhausted into bed.

I wrote more poems and journals about this—the loneliness—than anything else. I had to keep telling myself to "put one foot in front of the other"—a trite saying that came to have a vivid meaning for me because I was incapable of believing that I had a future. One foot was enough, was all I could handle, and it was a long time before I could observe any movement forward at all.

Each day, I searched desperately for the mail, listened acutely for the phone or the doorbell.

> May' 03
>
> *The depression is lifting a little, but with that comes the horrible sadness, facing the awful truth that he is never coming back. I can't do it. And then I discovered, with Pao Yu's help that I'm missing my self. I am not my self, my old confident, busy, independent self. I have no confidence. I creep from little task to little task, and I am so terribly dependent: on the little white pills every night, every night; on friends who come and pick up the pieces of me that are scattered all over the floor and try to put them back together to form a semblance, a stick, of me. I have to help with that. I'm being carried, like a lump in a blanket, by each of the friends and family who try to help. Where is the me?*
>
> *I can't touch him. I can't hold him. I can't hug him and kiss him and talk to him and laugh with him and get mad at him and look at him around the house, and go out with him and sit next to him in the car, and lie next to him in the bed. I can't ever again. I suppose it helps to write these words, but I can't read them back. They are too painful.*

This—the aching loneliness, the being alone—was the cataclysmic change. This is what puts widows apart from those who have lost mothers or friends or anyone who hasn't lived with them. The pain of day-to-day loneliness is a thing quite apart from the pain of missing him. Knowing that I was starkly alone seemed impossible to bear, and getting used to it was my biggest adjustment. I asked several of my friends if they knew anyone who would like to "rent" an office (the money was not what I needed)—someone retired perhaps, who would like to get away to work on projects. I never found anyone, but Cheryl, one of my walking buddies, told me about how successful she had been in taking into her home foreign students/researchers at the University of Detroit/Mercy, within walking distance from both of us. I called the professor whose name Cheryl gave me, and she said she would keep me in mind. Only a few weeks later, they sent me Ashu, a young chemistry Ph.D. from India by way of France.

Ashu had a sweet and nurturant disposition—just what I needed. It was comforting to have someone in the house, and he would even cook for me on occasion. Sometimes we would watch movies together. When he left almost a year later, I was at a point where I could manage on my own.

I did not—and do not—enjoy living alone, but I am no longer terrified or depressed by it. I don't like sleeping alone, or the solitary meals, or the quiet in the house, or not being able to share and talk over details of my life without getting on the phone to do so. I don't like going to events by myself (although I have done that in the past). I don't like having the total responsibility of the house, with its constant repair/upkeep, or the car, or the dog. In the first months, I simply couldn't do any of those things. But day by day, as my energy returned, I learned how. Gradually—very gradually as I did things—grumbling began to take the place of fear and helplessness.

anyone?

I'm looking for a man
now
gray heads turn mine
someone who is
cultured and thoughtful
reflective
someone who makes jokes
before
his eyes are open in
the morning
who
    handsome himself
tells me late
at night
that I was the best looking
woman at the party
with a deep social
conscience and
easy courage to
speak up
a bon vivant
well-loved by many
          many

not bloody likely

September 03

I tried not to feel too guilty for some of the feelings of this poem. I think it is more of a love poem than an advertisement. What also reassured me was the memory of my high school economics teacher who said once in class that the highest compliment one can pay to one's spouse is to remarry after losing her or him. I don't remember much about the economics he taught, but that idea has stayed with me over the years. (Funny that it should be so impressive, when I was worlds away from the experience at the time.)

And wanting to have a man in my life again has little to do with my love for Art. I have never, except for a few months, lived alone. So I miss the companionship, the affirmation. And the sharing—of politics, gossip, books, concerts—the exciting and the annoying experiences of our lives. I have learned to share these things with friends, but of course it's not the same. And I recognize, as in the poem, that I'm not going to find anyone like Art. As a woman in my 70s, I can see that the available pool of acceptable men shrinks to a trickle. That doesn't stop me from wishing.

Almost three years later, I did meet a man on the Internet. We met in person once, and I decided he was not for me. It was then that I learned something about myself: I am not desperate for companionship. That was a relief.

who we were

yin/yang I

if you are a saver and I am a thrower out
if I learn by doing and you learn by
 thinking
if I hear every note and you hear snatches
 and melodies
if you see tiny wildflowers in the forest
 microscopic urchins on the beach
 while I see forest and sea
if Sunday morning is your time for sleep
 and reading and my time to
 refinish furniture
if you are slow to anger/slow to call a truce
 and I am easily irked by small things
 quick to make up and forget
if I act too soon and you don't act soon
 enough
if you are so stubborn and I am so stubborn

why have we lasted so long?

1996

Art and I met in graduate school in 1970. He was an assistant professor of social work, teaching in the classroom and supervising students at a special children's rights unit with the American Civil Liberties Union. He had separated from his wife the summer before the term started, and was caring for his daughters, Lynn, 9, and Amy, 7.

I had gone back to school to finish my Bachelor of Arts in English., and was now applying for the School of Social Work at Wayne State University. My marriage was failing, but my two teenagers, Jim, 15, and Anne, 14, were central parts of my life and kept me there.

I was interested in civil liberties issues and had requested an internship at the ACLU. Art was an excellent supervisor of students, and for me, the stimulation and company of the other students assigned to the unit just added to the mix. We all liked him, loved his silly puns ("I'm going out for a chicken sandwich," he announced one day early in the semester, "if I can find the scratch.") A sense of humor has always been important to me, and I found myself liking this soft-spoken, principled, easygoing man. When we discovered that we had a mutual birthday (I was a year older), the students in the unit gave us a joint birthday party with a cake and wine. It was a great place to be, and we all worked hard.

A few months later Art and I found ourselves very much in love. We spent the next two years ecstatically happy together while we dealt with the tough problems of children, divorces and graduate school. I called it a roller coaster.

We were married in the Diego Rivera court of the Detroit Institute of Arts because we couldn't think of a more beautiful place to celebrate. When I mentioned to Art that, with the unusual venue of the wedding, the Detroit Free Press might want to cover it, he vehemently objected. I yielded immediately, and it was then that I found out just how private a person he was, making all the openness he shared with me so much more meaningful.

Art and I had a lot in common—active politics, social work of course, theater, travel, and a delight in entertaining friends at dinner parties. I cooked these dinners at first; but after all the kids had left home, he took up cooking and then took over the cooking (much to my delight). We lived simply but well and were lucky to have no major economic problems, so we ended up with a pretty carefree retirement income, a surprise to both of us. I mention this because it was especially important after he died. Many times I could afford to hire help for house chores that I had had no energy for.

Life was not all rosy. The problems of divorce morphed into problems of custody and a blended family, and some of these times were wretched. Eventually however we found ourselves in the empty nest. It was then that we began to travel, attend concerts and plays and museums, and generally enjoy ourselves.

Art was easy and agreeable to live with, and I found a freedom in our relationship that I had never known before. We had our differences of course. At one point, about ten years before he died, he announced to me, "Suzanne, I am simply not going to have any more fights with you about time." (He liked to get to engagements early, and I always found six other tasks I had to do just before we were supposed to leave.) I think now that he knew, after he had his first heart surgery, that he needed to reduce his stress, and time fights were stressful. Curiously, the effect that statement had on me was a change in attitude: I knew it was much harder on him to be late than it was on me to give up getting the jobs done, so we moved a little closer to agreement. He also told me once, shaking his head after I had left the house unlocked for the umpteenth time, "I'm gonna get you your own house." I learned to take seriously these apparently light remarks and try to adjust (it wasn't easy).

When grandchildren came along, Art was in his element. He was one of those devoted, loving, proud grandfathers that all grandchildren love to have around. He delighted in playing with them—on their terms, in their worlds—but always drew limits, and respected their parents' rules. Erik, Rachel and Ruby adored him.

The First Weeks

Art died on a Saturday night, and by early Sunday morning friends were coming in and out most of that day and the following. I talked to them, was grateful that they came, and carried on conversations because it was expected of me. I don't remember crying much then. We talked about him, and mostly I tried to console others, who were pretty devastated.

I spent the next several weeks preparing for the memorial service. Part of my professional life had included conference planning, and some of the skills I had came into practice. Years before, I had served as president of the local Funeral Consumers Society, where I developed a model for memorial services. I concluded, after attending many of them, that the best tribute to the loved one and the most enjoyable to attend for friends and family was the simplest: just ask everyone to get up and share their memories—and that's what we did.

The service was held in Central Methodist Church, although neither of us was religious. But this church was well-known in Detroit for its pacifist minister in the 1950s, for hosting Martin Luther King for his "I Have a Dream" speech, and for being the center of peace and justice demonstrations and gatherings for decades.

Meanwhile, I returned to my therapist. I did dozens of crossword puzzles and played hundreds of games of solitaire. My friends took me out. I saw my physician and got some mild sleeping pills. The high points of my days were opening condolences in the mail, checking my e-mail, talking to friends on the phone, and being able to go to bed and sleep.

I was retired, had no paying job to go to and had dropped all of my volunteer work. I made sure that no demands were being made on me when I had no energy to meet them, but still I wondered about younger widows I'd known who had to go off to a job where they could get their minds off their grief. I wondered also if the small children that they might be caring for were a similar distraction. But I also knew that jobs and children take their toll in energy-sapping and add to an already long list of burdens that come with loss.

I did have beautiful, supportive, helpful, thoughtful friends and family. They stayed overnight in the house with me, called me, took me for walks and movies and plays and concerts, brought me dinners, had me in their homes for dinners, and were there when I needed them most. They were friends that Art and I had made together. They knew us; they grieved for him themselves—we grieved together. In a strange way, Art by just being Art had helped prepare me for what I had to go through without him. But it became clear to me that the close, intense relationship we had made for a hard grieving.

(I wrote this poem for the memorial program)

For Thor

I have had the Hallelujah chorus
sung for me by a thousand voices
the Berlin Philharmonic in the pit
and Handel himself
on the podium

I have been
    after decades of languishing
    hopelessly within
    John Donne's unrequited
    love poetry
incredulously
gloriously
        requited

I have been carried to
Elysium by you
my Gentle Giant
with sumptuous banquets
set before me
and entertained by a command
performance of the Cirque de Soleil

it will almost be enough

(Anne Higgins is the sister of my friend Ellen Parrish. She kindly added me to the regular emails she send to her family.)

Dear family,
January 22, 2003

    When Ellen moved to Detroit 30-some years ago, she became fast friends with Suzanne and Art Antisdel and over the decades the rest of us did, too. Whenever we gathered at Ellen's, the lucky spill-over got to go down the block to the Antisdel's to spend the nights. Suzanne and Art as a couple were so gracious and delightful that hanging out with them was a treat. Their living room seemed emblematic of their lives, with a beautiful piano and wonderful art work, everything interesting and harmonious and reflecting their wide interests. They were smart, funny, multi-talented, politically passionate, and willing to invest time and money in what they believed— which were, for the most part, anti-war groups and causes. On top of everything else, Art was a superb cook. They would host soirees at their house, during which Ellen and Suzanne would give a four-handed piano recital, people who wanted to would recite poetry, and then everyone would fall in at the dining room table where Art had prepared a feast.

    It is with great sadness that I relate that last Saturday night, he died. He had had heart surgery the day before, complications had arisen, and he didn't make it. He certainly wasn't planning on dying. He'd already gone through two hip surgeries and a heart valve replacement, and I'm here to tell you that, either in spite of or because of the surgeries, he invited me to join him in a wicked lindy hop at Gregory and Tracy's wedding. When he knew he had to have a second heart operation, Suzanne e-mailed me that she was depressed but he wasn't. He was facing it with his usual serenity and optimism. She, as a matter of fact, printed out a funny book review I had sent her so she could read it aloud to him after the operation. I can't think of a better symbol of their lives together: to face the future, as they had the past, with devotion, conviction, and humor.

love,
Anne

changes

I want you back
but the fish you knew are dead
the dear dog you knew
and loved
and got annoyed at when
he did his breathy dance
around the kitchen table
when you were trying to read
the Times

is dead

we even have a new
tea kettle

september 03

parts of speech

my grammar is
inconsistent
I cannot get
accustomed
to   *I*
    and   *my*
        and   *was*

I misuse them
at the most
unexpected moments

this will never come
easily

September 03

impression

three women
who hardly knew you
were moved to tears
at Ruby's
Me and Pah
book

tears welled up in the eyes of
my yoga teacher
when I simply
told her how I
missed you

unintentionality
personifies you
you never really knew
how much you
moved other human beings

now
even after death

June 03

we had it all

we had it all
didn't we?
we had that
rare
combination
of two creatures
who loved
to the hilt
without
reservation
without threat
or defense
but wholeheartedly
trusting each other
to return
all we gave

and we knew
we knew
we had it
we knew
every second
that you
were the best thing
ever to happen
to me
and I to you

lucky us

December 03

Dear Suzanne -

I'm sure you've received notes such as this by the trunkload over the last few weeks, but permit me to express how deeply, deeply saddened I was over Art's death. From the time I met him the very first time I dined at your home in 1977, I came away impressed by his extraordinary graciousness, wit, and sincere desire to make one feel truly welcome.

On the numerous occasions over the intervening years when the two of you opened your doors to the Nichols family – the available slots in your spare bedrooms were vied over and I, being unabashedly spoiled, elbowed my way to the front of the line with not the slightest vestige of shame – the opportunity to enjoy the hospitality which you both so unselfishly extended was like being handed a free pass to the best B&B in town.

He was truly the sort of bon vivant ("entertaining" is the word that keeps appearing to me, high praise indeed in my mind) that made my visits to Detroit much anticipated and memorable. It was also so obvious to me that he loved you profoundly. I shall miss him. –

William Nichols

(Ellen Parrish's brother)

old habits

your picture
calls
tells me that
you would like to
be alive again
to comfort me
and dance with me
again
and this time
you'd still
not get the air
out of the ziploc
bag
before you close it

I wouldn't mind

July 04

Dear Suzanne,

I'm sorry I didn't get a chance to hug you at the memorial service. I loved the stories your family told about him. I have one of my own. When he retired I asked him what he was going to do now. He told me, now he could afford to piss people off (his words). I loved that statement!

Pat Cason-Merenda

(a fellow Detroit activist)

equilibrium

we were
yin and yang baby
Hamlet's answer
you were
I did
a teeter totter in motion

the little arguments
big fights
silent periods
delicious sex
the love notes
and little gifts for
no occasion
the intensive talks or
quiet knowing you were
there
in the house
suzart on the pillows
yin and yang baby

January 04

...he was a good citizen of the world
                              Peggy and Sam Tundo

(Detroit Symphony Orchestra members; Peggy and I had performed a Beethoven sonata for violin and piano for friends one Sunday, along with neighbor Alvin Aubert's poetry reading and Art's wonderful food.)

bed

from our first nights
I slept on your right
at home
or traveling

I do so now
fading gently the
secret strong
hopes
denials
beliefs
that you'll come back to
fill the empty space
a hard habit to break
and no need to
anyhow

January 04 ogod

shoeshine I

you there in the bedroom
chair
surrounded by the
rags and brushes
and spitting
in the right place
at just the right
moment
I haven't mastered that

doing it for myself
doesn't hold the
magic of
your gift of
love

January 04

shoeshine II

I shined my shoes
today
all by myself
they were looking so
 shabby
I had to do something
or stop wearing them
I did a passable job
but they never
quite achieved that
gleam

January 04

doing without

doing without you
is like
doing without music
in my life
like being deaf
(a lifelong fear)
and never hearing
heavenly
surprising
chord changes

the world of
humans bringing me
tonal feelings
with their voices
    or instruments

out of my ken now

september 03

not

There will come a time when
I don't think about
wanting you back

won't there?

September 03

    I thought so often of having him back. I couldn't resist the dream. I would promise: "just for one day" (like dead Emily in "Our Town," who is taken back to her family kitchen on her 16th birthday). But if I agreed to such a restriction, I would have to lose him all over again, and I knew I could not withstand the unbearable pain—not even for one day of having him there again. The fantasy gave me comfort for a while, until I saw how much I would have to pay for it.

    At the time of this writing, I continue to put off viewing some of the videos my son made of Art. I know they're there, and I find it comforting, like a little savings account that I may never have to spend.

afternoons

now
some of the pain
abates
and I can think
again
look back
at long
too short
afternoons
in your bed
when I could get away
to lovemaking
as I had never
known it
until then

the air was pink
with excitement
    pleasure
        deepening of love
melting into you
until it was
my bed
too

March 04

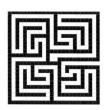

THE FOG

things

The house—the home—was important in our lives. Here we worked hard to make it beautiful for us to live in and to share with our friends. It is a big old house built in 1929, situated in a once-fashionable section of Detroit where upper-middle class Detroiters once lived in comfort with live-in servants and two-car garages. When we moved there in the '70s, the neighborhood was still rather middle-class and racially mixed—black and white. It has remained so, with strong community ties and activities. We were always close to many of our neighbors, both as acquaintances and friends.

Inside the house, there were numerous objects that we had lovingly acquired to brighten our lives: items from our travels—junky things we brought back to life (this was an enjoyable hobby of mine), gifts we found for each other. In each of these there were memories: of struggles to find time after work to do house chores, of trips taken, of the simple and complex process of living together, sharing space and knowing the other was here.

And it was here that I spent all of my grieving time in the first months, afraid or reluctant to go out, except when kind friends took me with them to events. So I was confronted constantly with reminders—individual objects and the aura of the house itself.. The pain of memories was unbearable at first. It was several months before I could remember without hurting. When eventually I could, it was with a kind of sad joy, to pull him back to me in my imagination.

The bed of course was the focal point, the center of everything, where I cried the most, where I would stroke his pillow, where I felt his absence most painfully. It had been, of course, the location of beautiful sex, conversations of intimacy or just everyday stuff, sometimes a place of icy anger. And it was here that, just before the final surgery, he took on the habit of whispering "Good night, my sweet babboo." I knew then as I knew later that he was doing it to create a good memory for me.

A friend told me she had her daughter, 12, sleep with her for a few months until she could handle sleeping alone. My cousin Mavis, after several months a widow, confided that she was still sleeping on the couch because she could not bear to sleep in the bed where she and her husband had shared so much.

milestone

I washed your
last towel yesterday
just tossed it down
the chute as if
it were any old towel
and not the one you
had touched
had been wrapped around
your precious
warm
body

I'm frightened now
that memories too
will
become meaningless

September 03

memento

I've kept the
last
pillowslip
you used
wrapped up in a
plastic bag
high on a shelf
in the linen closet

I'm sure all the
smell of you is
gone by now
but what's the point
of unwrapping it

May 04

fixing

they seem to know
these silent
tools and
places for our
living
that one of us
is gone

that the other
stands inside
also broken
but unrepairable

January 04

furnishing

this table
a long oak came
I think
from a library sale
sat for years in
the basement
patiently shabby
used for pounding
nailing
storing paint

one day it
shone out at me
and I shined it back
installed it in the
breakfast room

we talked and
ate here
your good food
stimulating talk

now it's getting
gently dented
by the endless slap
of playing cards

October 03

mailbox

the little red
plastic mailbox
moves
on my dressing table
a Valentine once
filled with cheap
little candy hearts
with silly love
messages
you bought it for me
and I'm sure you
gave me
with it
a handmade
paper valentine
with a delicious salacious
message

now it moves
an inch or two
from where I've
deliberately placed it
testing

it could be the dog
bounding up the stairs
shaking the old house
or
might it possibly
be you
playing with me
again?

January 04

    I never got over wanting him back. At first, I tried to put aside my agnosticism to make room for his being somewhere, where I could retrieve him, bring him back to live here.

house past tense

after a relatively
good day
    no crying
    no surges of sadness
    not thinking
I come down the stairs
screaming
    Look at this house!
        I liked living here
      with him
          I liked it!

July 03

the attic

cleaning out
the attic
I reread our
love letters

long ago
they had been tucked into
my student box
or your faculty
box
surreptitiously
     we thought

they were full
of love
and excitement
and longing
and surprise at
each other's
love

I never got over
the surprise

May 03

clothes

your clothes are
still in the closet
hanging

I brush past them now
where before
I could
not move past them
burying my face
in your shirts
hunting
hunting
for your smells
anything

July 04

the closet

Okay.
I'm ready
I think I'm
    ready
to give away
your clothes
and your shoes

what will I do with
all that closet
    space?
I was not meant to
live alone in
this house
I'm still not
comfortable not
sharing the bathroom

I remember seeing
a deeply
poignant scene in
an Alec Guinness movie
he has
lost his wife
and stands in the closet
and draws her clothes
to him
and weeps
burying his face in one of
her dresses

I cried then
not knowing
it would happen
to me

May 04

(In 2006, I was still trying to get myself to give away the rest of his suits.)

Dear Suzanne,
Thanks for honoring Micah and me with Art's shirts and sweaters. This week-end, his shirts went to a peace meeting, a freedom school meeting and a School of the America's meeting. Art would be proud and his legacy continues.

love,
Rich

(Rich Feldman is Janice Fialka's husband and a dear friend and fellow activist. Micah is their remarkable son.)

I was in a fog for what seemed like months, and I slowly came to realize that it was protective. I could not have borne the reality of death—I could not have lived with it. So I kept it at bay for months, until I regained, little by little, enough energy to deal with it. One of my friends, a Nicaraguan woman visiting here, told me that when I was ready, I should "change the furniture around." It took me a few months to understand what she was talking about.

The gradual acceptance of this dreaded reality was one of the longest and most demanding processes of all.

When I wrote this next poem in 2001 we had no intention of moving, but this was a good way to write about how much we loved being here.

to the new owners of our house

Be sure to follow the colors
across
the kitchen each morning
as the sun penetrates
the stained glass
projecting green and yellow
on the wall

and savor the surprise
when it suddenly shines directly
on the upstairs landing greenery
early spring

but you'll have to
sit helplessly as
despite
your careful plans each year
the garden surprises you

don't forget to chuckle/smile/frown
together
over memories of last night's
dinner party conversations,
lying lazily in bed of a
Sunday morning

drink in the birds!
sparrows elbowing each other
out of the way
of the lifegiving feeder
or finches sitting steadily
nibbling on the thistle
they've passed the word
this is a good place
for handouts

some nights you might want
to take dinners
at the coffee table to
enjoy the fire

do catch the trees budding
from the
special vantage point
of the third floor skylight
and when you sweep
the snow from that pane
listen for the gentle
plop
as it hits the ground

if you have a Barca
use the basement
landing to wipe each paw
when he comes in
from surveying his muddy
territory
he will expect it
sit
and wait for it
you may make a different
set of
friends and enemies here
both are a sign that
you are not afraid to
try to get close

oh...and
there are fireflies in the
back garden
you can see them from
the porch swing

but even if they don't
show
it's good to sit on the
swing
turn out all the lights
    and wait

holidays

Holidays are the worst...people would tell me. They were mostly referring to "the holidays"—Christmas, Hanukkah and New Years. And they were terrible. Many widows I've spoken with agree with that. And there was some solace in believing that "just getting through the first year, getting through the first holidays, the birthdays, without him..."—having passed the worst, the next year just had to be better. It is a desperate clinging to hope that sometimes works.

For me, there was no miraculous change when the first anniversary of Art's death was passed. It simply didn't get much better, and I really hadn't expected that to happen. My grief had a life of its own that simply had to be lived out. It died when it chose to, and it didn't consult me.

But holidays usually mean families getting together, and there, in that empty chair or the empty space, is the reminder. With supportive families like mine, we talked about him, talked about the empty space, talked about our own sadness, and it helped. It helped me and everyone in the room—even those who didn't talk much about their feelings. Starting sentences with "Art would have loved this..." brought out all kinds of memories, and somehow then, he would be there. We brought him into the gathering, the celebration, the joyous commemoration, dampening the joy a little, but in sharing the moment we shared the grief, and it was always a relief.

plans for hanging on

I'm doing all that I can
whatever I can
to manage the back pain
to hold grief at bay
to distract
divert
plan for times with others
especially in January
to have lots of plan Bs
to resist depression
    and anxiety
to take not enough pills
    to make me a zombie
to watch movies
and any good tv I can find
      even the commercials
to do crosswords
and play solitaire
    without sitting

to get out of bed
in the morning
and take a step

December 03

avalanche

it all comes at once
our birthdays
the holidays
the death anniversary

I was doing all right
actually seeing a
little progress
then this

I want to fly to Mars
I want to fast forward to
February

too much to bear
can't run far enough away
can't deal with it
just hanging on
wishing days away

forgetting how
precious life is

December 03

holidays

I made it through
Thanksgiving
and our wedding
anniversary
I would like to
skip over
our birthdays
and
Christmas
jump over the
calendar days
like a giant hopscotch
board
and
into the empty
sidewalk
beyond

December 03

anniversary

the Day has come and
gone
the supporters came
and went
some remembered with me
all the terror of a year ago
it was no big deal
I didn't hurt
any more this day
than any other
a yarzeit candle
lit your picture
but all we did and said
didn't bring you back

January 04

condolences

Opening envelopes or email, or answering the phone was lifegiving to me. I desperately needed to hear the shock, the sympathy, the memories, the offers to help that each one contained. They helped me through my own shock, my own sympathy for Art and my sympathy for myself.

These condolences recount their own memories of Art and tell me how they are grieving with me. And they sympathize, empathize, offer support. They try to console. As the mail came each day, I treasured every card, even if it was printed and with only a signature. The ones I treasured and reread, of course, had personal notes. (This was yet another reminder of friends who didn't know what to say, so they said nothing, and I came to understand them in time.)

As is always the way, the farther away the letters came from, the more surprised I was and the more comfort they gave me. One always expects one's friends to be supportive, bless them, but surprise coupled with the sympathy was a treat. I try to remember that when I hear of the deaths of people not close to me.

Of the many I received, I've sprinkled a few throughout these pages.

regrets

Readers whose loved ones died slowly, with cancer or another degenerative disease, may have had a different experience from mine—that of a sudden death. But whether they, like me, deny it to the end or not, it makes no difference. In my denying, I denied myself the final goodbye, something I regretted immediately and still think about. But I do know this: there is no perfect way of doing it.

I thought I had always valued and acted with honesty and forthrightness—speaking one's mind, confronting the issue, relieving the tension of secrecy. But in the case of Art's illness, I discovered that I had done my share of denial by simply not allowing such an unacceptable idea as death to enter my mind, much less our conversation. He did not deny; he had lived with the threat of death for about seven years since his first heart surgery. And he was accepting—something I could not be.

But there are other regrets, and they are common: Did I tell him I loved him? Did I treat him well? Did I appreciate him? What about that mean-spirited remark I made during the heat of an argument? Or that uncaring behavior when I didn't do something that I knew meant a lot to him, like calling him if I was going to be late?

> April 03
>
> *I've been reading bits of Without, Donald Hall's poetry after his beloved wife Jane Kenyon died. He says that to be aware of the bliss would have made him afraid to lose it. I think that's where we were—not aware at all of the bliss.*
>
> *But I did experience the fear—it was what sent me to my therapist [Corinne]. I didn't know it at the time—I went because I was unhappy with the way I was treating Art. It took me a year to realize that I was making preemptive strikes—totally unlike me. I will distance you from me before you can die and distance yourself from me, so I will not be hurt.*

> *He was so very relieved to hear this explanation when I told him about it, after almost a year and a half of therapy. It must have been so hard for him to wait until I was ready to let him know, but that was his nature. We had a beautiful year after that.*

For most of these doubts I was able to convince myself that I had more or less been a good lover and wife. The big question for me was: Did he know how much I loved him? I thought of countless opportunities missed, so many times I could have said or done something to show him. But I later came to realize that the real question was: Did I know these things? Was I fully aware of how much he meant to my life? The reassurances of friends and family helped, but it took time to convince myself that there was nothing, really nothing now, to regret.

reassurance

after some time
I can see that
the feelings were just
    there
without words
or gestures
without my awareness
they lay
steadily
beaming their
electricity
between us

January 2006

freedom

I envy other widows
a bit
their sense of relief
to do what they want
now

no relief for me
with you I have
always
done what I wanted
chosen what I wanted

used to acceptance I
have been what I am
freedom was never
a consideration with
so much of it at
my disposal

I hope it was mutual
though I could never tell

December 03

doubt

I think you knew
I loved you

I think you were
    as I was
comfortable
enough that you
no longer thought about it

I can only turn
to others now
and ask them to convince me
which of course leaves me
unconvinced
because I had to ask

July 2004

music

essence

Blossom Dearie
sings
the song is funny
but she
    sitting back
    with a sideways
    view
      one eyebrow raised
      and only the trace
      of a smile
is funnier than
the song

in the car
I weep

life with Blossom
is so so full
of precious
  perfect
  delightful
moments of
stunning sunny
clarity

and he is missing it

August 04

good jazz

good jazz at
ten o'clock
a martini
at five
or coffee at
six pm
dancing in the kitchen
biorhythms and
clocks coinciding
falling into pink
clouds

September 02

lyrics

our thirty years
spill over
to now
so I can still have you

hearing love
songs on the radio
convinces me
that despite my current
need for some man
in my life
there will never be
anyone else

February 05

August 15, '03
Cape Cod

Depression has lifted quite a bit

Anxiety is still here—hard to get to sleep – suspect pills are no longer working. Trying to find workable methods and strategies.

Missing him, still terribly, especially when music standards are played on this Cape station, and there are lots of friends and family to help reminisce.

Music has always been important in my life; I was a precocious musician with perfect pitch who plinked out tunes when I was two, they tell me. And Art loved both jazz and early music. Concerts and a small collection of recordings were an essential part of our lives. We didn't always share tastes, so I would attend chamber music concerts without him, but usually we went together. For several years before we met, I played piano in small clubs to earn money for school or the house or the kids. I have always had a fondness for cabaret songs—the standard popular tunes of Gershwin, Cole Porter, Jerome Kern, Richard Rogers et al, and later, Stephen Sondheim. Well-written lyrics that go well with the tune are especially important, and I love to play them as well as listen to vocalists like Mel Torme or Sinatra or Sarah Vaughan and others, who know just how to put over a song with sensitivity and taste and musical emotion. Often at family gatherings I would play some of these songs, and on the rhythmical ones Art would jump in on his bongo drums, enhancing the music as well as the mood. (He was very good but very modest.)

For the memorial service, I chose Jerome Kern's "The Folks That Live on The Hill" and a particular favorite of Art's, 'When Sunny Gets Blue." They brought tears to my eyes then, and do so now, as do countless other tunes. And often, especially in the early months, I would find myself singing along with especially haunting tunes and lyrics, like "I Concentrate on You," "I'm Glad There is You," "Where Are You?" and "It Never Entered My Mind" –songs of love and loss and loneliness. And Chet Baker's lonely muted trumpet wailing to "These Foolish Things" needed no words to move me to tears. I did a great deal of crying in the car, a habit I shared with many widows, I discovered.

And at home, with the radio on for a good part of the day, I would weep instantly hearing these love songs. Even at this writing, when Art has been gone for almost three years, certain songs sung with sensitivity can melt me into a puddle. The power of good music, I think, lies in its ability to reach your gut, send chills through your body and lift your soul. A grieving heart, so emotionally vulnerable, is especially open to all these effects.

In that grieving season, the pain was sometimes unendurable. Now it is sweet and I welcome it. I hope I shall always be vulnerable in this way.

time

time out

now
is waiting for
good

at the beginning of
a bright stretch
hoping to
slow it
from becoming
the dreaded
     then

and now is
looking back
at the terrifying
clutched in its
inescapable horror
until
closing the eyes and
turning the head
it is shut out
until the next
now

November 03

no date

now that the year is
up
I clutch the idea of
    season

widowhood season

loss season

no date is
set for its end
until I set it
retroactively

April 04

Time became lost for me. It was as if I were unconscious and coming up for short periods of awareness. Some of the awareness of time came with writing, but lasted briefly. I would forget I had done things or what I had told people. I rarely knew what day it was without looking at the calendar or asking someone, and I made countless mistakes in scheduling. The calendar didn't help much; I would note engagements on the right day of the wrong week. I had little grasp of when things had or had not happened. And it bothered me only a little. I seemed to be comfortable in a timeless universe, drifting from hour to hour, day to day without a past.

When the worst of the grief was behind me, I could identify past dates by pre-death or post-death. I think I may always think this way, dividing my life into three: the black hole of about a year and a half (the most intense months of my grieving), my life before it happened, and the period from when the healing began. "How long ago did you get those drains reamed out?" a workman asks me. As with all such questions, I see a long passageway, with darkness around that year-and-a-half, and light on either side of it. Only then can I count years. His death is the watershed, the identification point around which everything else happens.

pets

As someone naturally affectionate, I felt the loss of Art in many ways, not the least of which was the loss of someone to be physically close to. I would often kiss him casually as I passed him in one room or another. And whenever we were driving together, I would reach over often and pat his thigh. With nothing else to do in the car, it was an easy gesture when I remembered how much I loved him. He would always return the affection, or initiate it himself.

Art was in and out of the hospital several times and required my care, which I gave willingly and gladly. And when he was well, we cared for each other in little ways. Not having someone to care for when he died left a deep void in my life, and I was grateful for the dog—and even the fish— to help take up that space. All the dogs I've had throughout my life have loved being petted and getting the praise that goes with affection. But perhaps more important to me in my grief, dogs need care.

And a dog can be a godsend when one is grieving. She is a companion in a lonely house. She will listen when you talk to yourself, and will love you no matter what (I'm reminded of the bumper sticker that says "Please help me to become the person my dog thinks I am"). She will follow you around the house whenever you are home and will understand much of what you say to her. A dog is a grateful recipient of any attention you want to send her way. Depending on the breed (mine have always been Labrador Retriever mixes) she can sit still for an unlimited amount of petting, hugging and kissing. She responds; her tail wags in greeting you back into the house. My dog's tail wags when I talk to her, or even when I can laugh. She gets me out to walk when I don't feel like it.

Barca

"Too lively" was the condemnation on
the cage where he waited
having worn out two owners
(a puppy's heart
inside a big ungainly body
his floppy ears
    huge paws

        great sweeping tail
more than he could control)

And when he came to us
he was aloof
not expecting much.

We had lots of caring we
wanted to shower on him
wanted to hug and
talk tender
rub his soft fur and
hear his grateful grumble

It took some time for him
to trust
to believe he could stay.
Maybe he learned that
we needed him.

             1996

April 4, 03

Tuesday. I lost it with Barca. First I had had a terrible crying jag, started by whoknowswhat, and I called Anne. Talking to her calmed me down, especially when Ruby came to the phone and asked, "Are you having a lonely day?" Then a few hours later, Barca started acting out, humping his bed into a hump so he couldn't lie on it, dragging each of the 3 or 4 kitchen rugs all over the house, then coming to me several times after I had settled in to vegetate at the tv and asking to go out, come in, fix his bed so he could again lie on it, etc., etc. I have no patience, no resources to deal with these things. If I had had a knife I would have killed him, maybe. I turned to the counter and screamed and screamed, "I can't do this! I can't do this!" Then I called Janie who screamed "What's the matter?!" and then said she'd be right over. Which she was, about half an hour later. I gave her a pair of Art's old pajamas and she stayed the night.

Late in the springtime of 2003, Anne drove here with her dog, on one of her many visits that year. And one afternoon, she piled both dogs, her Morgan and my Barca, into her station wagon for a run in the park When it was time to go, she called the dogs to get in the car, and as soon as she slammed the hatchback door down, she realized that she had locked the keys inside. From there, everything went wrong. The lock service that came with her car never arrived; I was in the shower and didn't get her call to me for a good hour; when I got there, it took us, usually takecharge women but now grieving and not functioning up to par, a long time to take action. Meanwhile, we could see the dogs in distress, especially Barca. When I saw him foaming at the mouth and pawing the air, I grabbed a brick to throw into the window. Just then, the police arrived and did it for me, but it was too late for Barca. The policewoman took him immediately to the vet, but he died on the way. Morgan, after cooling down with wet towels, recovered.

It was horrible. Anne felt wrenchingly guilty, and losing Barca just added to the grief for both of us. Friends gathered around us, just as they did after Art died, especially the dog lovers, who could empathize more than others. But the fact remained: here was another loss. We grieved together, and when Anne left to drive home, she left Morgan with me, understanding full well how a dog can help just by being there. I felt I had been dealt a double whammy.

A couple of months later, I found Barclay-the-hound on the internet. He was beautiful, but damaged, and I didn't find that out until I took him home. He jumped fences, high and low; chewed everything in sight; stole food; barked insistently, shrilly at me for most of his needs, and generally drove me nuts. I tried everything I could think of, but he never improved. And more important, I had no resources to deal with him. I took him to obedience school, something I had never had to do for my previous dogs. The training was fine, but other than learning a few commands, neither of us improved much with the experience. Things got worse and worse and I found myself crying hysterically in frustration several times a week. After six months of this, I gave up and concluded that he would have to be put down. I couldn't pass him on to anyone else—for his sake as well as the new owner's—so I had no other recourse.

lax training

Barclay you're
lying on the
oriental rug
I wouldn't have
allowed it
before
but now
I'm so grateful for
the mutual dependency

August 03

September 10

I have just had three horrendously stressful days. I got through them by the skin of my teeth and by not noticing how bad they were. Until now.

Tuesday I took the Prius in for what I thought would be a simple wheel alignment. One thing led to another, and I ended up waiting around all day. Stress. I came home to some (again) annoying and stressful insurance decisions (I'm beginning to hate that word).

On both Monday and Tuesday, Barclay pooped on the dining room oriental. Today I lost it entirely and haven't spoken civilly to him in the last 2 hours. I finally took a tranquilizer, by the time Annie called and I told her that I was throwing in the towel, and that Barclay really isn't the dog for me, I could tell her in a less than hysterical voice. He's a hell of a challenge to anyone, but to someone who is not altogether mended from the worst blow of her life—no. He's simply too much for me to handle. But what shall I do with him?

(On rereading this journal, I wonder if that dog might have been managed by someone in better shape. Granted, he was really difficult, but again, I had no resources, no strength or energy to deal with even the smallest problems, and that dog demanded too much of me.)

putting the dog down

I had
one whole painless
day
a few days ago
then this

a pall is cast on
all my thinking
all my doing
and this time
I don't have
fog
to soften it

February 04

dog gone

that funny rustle of
something in
the next room—
it's not the dog

my ear must get
accustomed to
new sounds now

February 04

the leaving

I couldn't get his
eyes to close
he had peed
all over the blanket—
just let go

finally

February 04

My friend Janie went with me to the Humane Society, and we both cried over him. He was a beautiful, intelligent animal that had experienced, somewhere in his life, a trauma that left him so neurotic I felt he was worthless as a pet. It was again another loss for me.

It wasn't until several months later that I was ready to get another dog. This time I had moved out of the throes of deep grieving and I could choose more carefully. Keller, a young female Lab mix, turned out to be one of the dearest additions to my life. She sleeps on the floor of my bedroom and I can talk to her all day when I'm home. She's very protective and responsive to my affection. We fill each others' needs. Art would have loved her.

self-image

cordoned off

in the supermarket
I walk the aisles
self consciously
seeing myself as
cocooned in a fog
cordoned off
untouchable

I am untouchable
not to be held
responsible
weak as a sylph
as a phantom
gliding down the
Breakfast Cereals
   aisle
emerging momentarily to
pay
real money
at the checkout
counter

April 04

commonalities

my dog peed on
another dog
at the dog park
today the owner
was not gracious
I was at a loss

he's fragile
like me
too many homes
no real trust yet
he's hyper
I'm anxious

July 03

change the view

slowly
laboriously
alone
on a hollywood
movie set
a street
with enormous
heavy
building facades
empty of depth

mine must be turned
to face an entirely
new direction
slowly pushing
laboring mightily
head downward
in concentration
I turn it
inch by inch

April 04

movement

something has changed
I'm not sure what
not me
not you
something

June 03

now I can...maybe

now I can maybe
take my place
take on some tasks
respond to what's asked
    of me
or what I ask of me

other widows I'm not
I still don't fit in
with your group

March 04

progress

reading my poetry
at home again
after three days
on the train across
Canada
with its friendly
Canadians
and breathtaking
vistas
I could see:

I've gathered ground too

October 04

Much of my self-image emerges in other poems—in the sections on depression, on loneliness, in others.

The image I remember most vividly is that of myself in the supermarket. Once while I was shopping I caught a glimpse of another woman who looked a little like me, as I see myself. She wore pants and a turtleneck (my uniform), and was passably attractive.

I kept thinking of her as me, as others see me, as I see myself. And I found it helpful to see this woman, functioning, going about her task of shopping, acting as if she were normal and like everyone else. But inside she was dying of grief. It helped me to form a perspective of who I was. I didn't need to take the image any further than just the woman shopping. It was enough.

The train trip across Canada was my watershed. I had thought about it earlier, when I was desperate for diversion:

> April 12 2003
>
> *This is Saturday night. I came up to check the email, do a few computer things, and finish my martini. Saturday nights have always been sacrosanct to us—even if we didn't do anything, we were always together and it was a special time. Most nights were spent entertaining or going out to friends'. I knew how much people liked to come here—now I have to think about how much people will still like to come here, but without Art. Without Thor, without him..*
>
> *I am looking into a future of loneliness. The house echoes with his voice, his presence, his love, his enjoyment of me, his enjoyment of life. I know I have to fashion a totally different kind of life for myself, and I just can't get my mind around it. I'm not ready to plan that concretely. Right now, I can only creep, like a baby. Tonight, I thought I could install a new CD drive—then I retreated to just reading a little of The Lion the Witch and the Wardrobe.*
>
> *I'm glad I have Barca, problems and all. He's troublingly acting out—missing Art too—and I haven't the resources to deal with him. I do try to be patient, but I'm not very good at it.*
>
> *There are glimmers of hope and light—I get ideas of traveling on the train from Toronto to Vancouver and visiting friends on the west coast. Just the thought of such a trip is a*

good sign. But then I know I have no energy to even consider it this summer.

Diversion, distraction, anything to build my energy while I'm plowing my way through this awful bog, up to my hips in heavy mud and not really sure which way I want to go even if I could get there easily anyway.

I think I'm in a stage where the depression is lifting a little (remember? The depression , the grief was one thing; missing him seemed to be a thing apart). Now I just miss him. Terribly, painfully, alone. The missing him comes when I'm alone, so I have no one to cry with, no one to hold me while I cry. Rochelle, the woman who came to guide me in yoga meditation, had tears in her eyes when I was crying and telling her about Art. Sadness begets pain begets sorrow begets tears. She doesn't know me, didn't know Art—and still she cried. Loss, of some kind, is universal. But I still have this feeling whenever anyone tells me, "Oh, yes, I lost my sister—or my mother…" that your loss can't possibly be as all-encompassing as mine. So all-encompassing that I can't go out, except to force myself out, and inside the house I'm just setting up diversions for myself so I won't cry. I have to, as Stanley said, walk that lonesome road all by myself. I can tell people about the suffering, but I have to suffer by myself.

…but the train trip didn't materialize until September 2004. Over the months, I had kept looking in my budget book at the column "Art's fund." He had done some consulting a year before, and had wanted to put away a cache to "do something with" some day. It never got spent, and after he died, I would glance idly at it each month as I paid bills. In the summer of 2004 I began to think about things I could do with that $1200. When I called Canadian Via Rail, they told me that the trip across the continent, with my own little roomette, would come to about $1200 US. I'm not one for "signs" but if I were, that would have been a good one.

The food on the train was great, the scenery spectacular, and the people friendly. I talked to a lot of them about losing him, since that was the reason for my trip. And I found many sympathetic ears, people who listened, encouraged, hoped for my future. When I came back home I felt as if I had completed a chapter. It wasn't until several months later that I looked back and realized I had stopped thinking of myself as a recent widow, had stopped introducing myself as Suzanne-I-have-just-lost-my-husband. It was then and only then that I felt that my season of grief had come to an end. Not the loss or the love or the memories, but the season of heavy, overwhelming mourning. I have heard many widows quote the adage, "You don't ever get over it; you just learn to live with it." Those words, after so many months, finally became real and meaningful to me.

The process of grieving gave me new insight into the issue of self-consciousness/awareness, both of myself and us-as-a-couple. At first I had no identity, no self-image. I had simply lost myself. Eventually, I saw myself as a widow. Please pity me—I have lost my dear husband. (There are many widows who fear being pitied. I needed to be pitied—or at least have my grief recognized. Once that was done, I could go on to talk about other things.)

Much later, I regained my identity, became me—a vastly changed me—but myself nevertheless. It was a little like an amnesiac who has to build herself anew, almost from scratch.

In addition, I had to work through the problem of how much we were aware of our love—its depth and breadth and excitement—and if I had valued it enough.. I thought about this much more after Art died than I ever did while he was alive. But I came to see how much not being aware (which in my grief I thought of as an omission, a regret, something I desperately missed) was not only a very human condition, but actually an advantage. I came to realize that being self-conscious—being aware of both our feelings for each other and how those feelings might have impressed others—would have robbed them of their spontaneity. And more important, it would have drained energy from us—the energy we were using for those feelings. In my grief I took an arduous journey searching for self-awareness that led me back out into an acceptance of simply being, of simply feeling. Self-consciousness is valuable sometimes, but not here.

travel

Travel could be called "running" in the early days. I traveled to be with my children, and I traveled to be with another widow. Anne and I traveled to Florida for a week, both of us to get away.

In the first few months, I was afraid to go out alone. I could go with others—to hold my hand, a metaphor that I used often, for going anywhere or doing a task that I dreaded. I don't remember how I got my groceries. But there were several times when I needed to have someone with me to get to a store to buy a simple item.

I was naturally drawn to other widows. In September, I took the train to Chicago to visit my friend Val. She had lost her husband almost a year before, so we had shared many tearful, helpful conversations about mutual grief, both on the phone and in email. I needed to see her, to commiserate, to just be with someone who understood so well what I was going through. (Group therapy, however, has never been my choice of support. I briefly considered joining a widow support group but discarded the idea.)

And I have always loved trains. They offer solace, comfort, interesting and changing views, other people to talk to—or not—and the rhythmic sound of the engine moving that giant locomotive. And especially, in my pre-grief days, they have offered a respite from responsibilities, where no phones are ringing and there is no way I can attend to tasks. So I can read or dream freely.

So it was when I boarded that train. Val was equally glad to see me. We had a lovely three days together, and I was perfectly at ease for that short time.

not yet

there is fog here
along the
train track
fog over the fields
in the woods
floating across the
little streams and
rivers
a comfortable fog
I am content and
cautious
under a cloudy
sky
safe now
from the other place
of light
busyness
and work

content to
stay within the
fog
and wait

Amtrak to Chicago
September 03

Airflights, however, were another matter entirely. They gave me panic, fear, disorientation, memory loss On flights, I did the only thing I could think of to calm myself: I wrote.

Right after the memorial, Anne told me I ought to come to visit in Baltimore, where both she and Jim live with their families. For my first flight there, my friend Pao Yu drove me to the airport. I had bought a book of crossword puzzles, to divert myself and help me get to sleep. I took them on every plane trip during the first several months, and sometimes I would write journals in the fly pages, especially on the difficult flights.

> February 6 '03
> *I am frightened of leaving home. My home, my city and state. The plane is heading into the clouds and it's too late. I'm in between, in limbo. When Pao Yu dropped me off, I wanted her to come with me, hold my hand, pat my hand, hug me until I got to Anne. I didn't ask her with words, but she knew. And we both knew she couldn't—that I'd have to do this alone.*
>
> February 10 Baltimore
> *I think I need to go home on early - Friday or Thursday. I'm tired – caring for Ruby is tiring me – much as I love her and need her for distraction. Home has tasks and friends that I don't have here. Anne and John have their own activities, their own lives – I'm wanted here, I know, but I'm on the periphery. And I think I'll get a lot more rest at home. I'll call Corinne [therapist] tomorrow and get her advice. There's nothing to keep me here, after my visit with Erik and Rachel. Anne, John and Ruby have been wonderful to me—wrapping me in loving care— unconditional selfless love. But I need to go home.*
>
> *I don't recognize myself. This can't be happening to me. Depression disorientation helplessness confusion total weakness – more than that: what's the word for it? Destroyed.*
>
> February 13 (at home)
> *The flight to Baltimore was a nightmare. I was so frightened. I made it through the check-in but then the security guy found T's knife that I was taking to Jimmy. I began to cry. He loved that knife. Kept it with him at all times,*

even repaired it when it got old. I know he loved Jimmy, who gave it to him, like the son he never had.

I began to cry. "My husband just died, and I'm taking that to my son..." The guy was understanding and told me to go back and check my carryon backpack, with the knife in it, at the check-in counter. I remember standing there with my head down, asking the woman behind the counter for "Patience – I'm going to need patience." I'm sure she didn't know what was going on. I was breathing hard, but trying to breathe in through my nose and out – pooh! pooh! – through my mouth. (I want to take a yoga class soon. As soon as everyone leaves after the memorial. God, I'm scared of that time. Corinne will be there for me, as often as I need her, I can call for an appointment. I can call Janie, or Kathleen, or Janice to come over and stay all night, maybe. But I need the time alone to watch TV, to be drawn into a drama and out of my uncontrollable life. So what do I do? They will watch TV with me. Yes, they will.)

At the Baltimore airport my bag didn't come through, and I had to stand at the counter and go through all the questions for lost baggage, holding on to the counter as I answered. Then the counter attendant's phone rang, and she told me my bag was coming through now. The whole trip was a blur—the layover in Chicago, getting on two planes—all a blur. When Anne met me at the Light Rail station, I told her that I hadn't had anything to eat since 5 a.m. when I'd had coffee. Later I remembered that I had had a substantial breakfast in Chicago. Just a blur.

I was so so glad to see Annie and Ruby, and I immediately calmed down. I hadn't even thought to take a tranquilizer, which might have helped the anxiety of the flight. When I was leaving Baltimore, I remembered to do some prevention, and swallowed one on the way to the airport. It did help, but I don't remember anything about that trip, either.

Anne and John's house is my second home, and I feel loved and welcomed there. They want me to come and live with them. So does Ruby. I won't do that, but it is so heartwarming to know they mean it. Ruby said, when I left, "I don't want her to go."

I think I will go down and watch some old tapes of "All Creatures Great and Small." Actually, I have some errands to do, and need to take Barca to the vet's. I'll be busy. Good.

February 19
This flight is better because I took a magic pill. But I'm still in a fog, see nothing funny, just want to get home. Soon. I miss Barca and my home and my mail and my friends. And I hated to leave the kids – so very good to me – they love me a lot—very comforting. I miss him terribly.

March 16.
I'm afraid to go out on errands alone. Afraid or reluctant to leave the house. It's comfortable inside. I have to be urged to walk. Pat does her best to get me out. All friends are trying. I need to start yoga and swimming (I'm not doing any of my exercises) but have to push myself to arrange these things. Can't move off center/inside. Florida and Anne will make a change – a good one, I hope. Anne came Sunday noon and spent until a week from that Tuesday with me, driving from Baltimore – 10 days!

March 22—Florida
Up at 4, after playing solitaire last night until 11:30 after the play. Endless games of solitaire here – not so many at home because I'm busy with home chores and phone calls. And here I can talk to Anne while I play. She has been marvelous— cooking, planning, cajoling me into the ocean, and onto a bike. It is somewhat of a respite here, warm and removed. But the sorrow still comes winging at me out of left field, and we talk about him often and at length. Anne says she now knows something of grief, having lost two fathers – and watching me. And the grief of losing John is now more real for her to imagine. I never had the foggiest idea what it would be like. No one told me, and I could never anticipate it, thank god.

March 25 Orlando airport
I'm frightened again – Anne is gone (possibly to return if she can't get on standby) and I'm alone. It's 11:30, and my

plane leaves at 3:10. More than 3 hours of empty waiting. The fountain is making water noises and I can feel the water with my hand if I need to. But I'm afraid of the empty time, of the pressure of the business of flying. Chewing gum and x-words will help get me past the anxiety stage, and maybe calm me to deal with the empty hours of waiting. Then there is always the little magic pill. I'm afraid of the day, stretching before me 8 hours before I walk in the door to Barca, the house, to Janie. Don't talk about your fears of the war, Janie. I can only take dealing with my own grief fears now.

Every year since we were married, we have gone to Stratford, Ontario, to the Shakespeare Festival there. I am convinced that it has the best theater this side of New York. Our friends Stan and Barbara Bernstein and neighbors Jim Edwards and Pat Murray would come along, and we always enjoyed being together, eating excellent food and discussing the plays for hours on end. The first visit back to Stratford after Art died was hard.

coming back to stratford

good talk
in the car
warm day
good plays and food
ahead
up the stairs

at the b&b
my gaze falls on
the bed
we shared the year
before

and suddenly
I wish myself
anywhere else
anywhere
even in a small
rightwing
libraryless
town in the winter
without a sweater

September 03

stratford redux

Going again
to places where
we were together
I do not see
what I am
looking at

I remember only
you
there beside me
where there is
emptiness now

August 04

Driving by myself for an extended length of time was traumatic. Driving has never been a favorite endeavor. I use a car to get from one place to another, but take little pleasure in the process.

> Aug 5-7 03
>
> This week I decided to drive to Bayfield [a small town in Ontario on the shores of Lake Michigan] with the dog, somewhat on the spur of the moment. I am leaving for a week in Cape Cod with Anne John and Ruby at the end of the week, but I called Elisabeth and asked her if I could try out Barclay for a couple of days to see how he would act in their cottage. She was very warm and hospitable and invited me up.
>
> I had told Janice I was going, and was anxious about the 3½ hour drive, and she urged me to call her if I needed to. I got lost twice on the once-familiar way to Port Huron, and at one point felt threatened and overwhelmed by the sight of the orange-and-white cones narrowing my road along route I-94. They seemed alive—and menacing. It became too much, so I took the next exit and called Janice. A few moments into the call I was sobbing, and she simply listened and said "umm, umm." Then she talked with me, and I calmed down. "You were wise to call. A lot of people know what you're doing and are thinking about you." It gave me the same feeling that some people have when they imagine angels around them. I hung up and got back on the road.
>
> The visit was calming and Joe and Elisabeth are good company. Elisabeth had to leave, but Joe and I talked about Art, and about grieving, and about the memorial service, which Joe said ought to have been videotaped and shown on PBS.
>
> Joe cooked dinner for me, and we talked about his interesting family, among other things. Around 10 o'clock I couldn't keep my eyes open any longer and begged off. I could hear Joe still cleaning up the kitchen as I got into bed. Thinking of myself as a widow—damaged, weak—allows me to let other people take responsibilities. That's strange for me, but I don't argue with myself. I think I know that
>
> my role of dependent is temporary. The drive home was direct and uneventful. I'm glad I did this for myself.

August 9, '03 on the plane to Cape Cod

I'm better. I'm flying without pills. I'm talking, chatting animatedly with my seatmate. I sound like my old self. I don't yet feel like that, but I sound it. My energy level is still low (confined to 4-5 hours in the morning) and I get anxious easily. Two days before my departure, I was very anxious, about tasks, readiness, memory. But here I am, with everything I need, on my way to better times. If travel was traumatic in the first months, it became therapeutic with the Canada train trip. Then it became just travel for pleasure, to visit my kids and grandkids, and to venture overseas. In any of its aspects, it was an important indicator of my emotional state.

COPING

coping with depression

March 16.
I'm afraid to go out on errands alone. Afraid or reluctant to leave the house. It's comfortable inside. I have to be urged to walk. Pat does her best to get me out; all friends are trying. I know I need yoga and swimming (I'm not doing my floor exercises) but have to push myself to arrange these things. Can't move off center/inside. Florida and Anne will make a change – a good one, I hope.

The depression I underwent felt as if something amorphous, huge, dark and unknown had gotten hold of me and was controlling my thoughts and my ability to cope. The times when I was in the thrall of such a demon, fearing it and feeling completely helpless were my worst times. They didn't last long, but were terribly hard to bear when they descended.

In The Life of Pi, Yann Martel says that fear is your worst enemy. But the question then becomes: how does one deal with it once it takes hold?

These poems speak for themselves, written from the depths. But across that gray and cold landscape there are small pinpoints of hope and comfort—the tiny lights that kept me putting one foot in front of the other each day And eventually I did find little ways to cope.

gifts

solitaire diverts my mind
the cards do my aimless bidding
unfeelingly
(except: why is the
queen of diamonds
so sad?
and why the jack
of spades so menacing?)
with such partners
I am not solitary

the dog keeps me
company
gives me love and doglike
affection when I cry
and frightening
uncontrollable
anger when he
misbehaves

sometimes
even as a pacifist
I want to
kill him
really kill him

crossword puzzles
get me to sleep
until the pill takes over
I take the last clue
to solve in the interim
in my head
in the dark

house tasks
animal tasks
keep me diverted

where reading
did

a martini
is the only food
that tastes good
that brings mmmms
at the first taste

food
uninviting
when eaten alone
takes on color
and calories
when I eat with
others

friends and family
keep me moving
alive and sane
remembering
how holy
and wonder-ful
are
human beings

July 03

sunfire

my breakfast room window
draws my eye irresistibly
to the garden
with its splashes of yellow

brilliant yellow finches
sometimes five or six of them
sit intently at the feeder
allowing me to gaze on
their holy beauty
at my leisure

they sit for minutes as I watch
one on the windowsill
wondrously close
waits for a sparrow to
vacate the perch

then beyond
four yellow tulips
and far beyond
at the back of the garden
forsythia in delicate display

this is a freely-given gift
from early morning
to after seven now
as I sip my martini
and drink in the scene
gulp it in

there is life here
to clutch
anything
that smacks of life
anything

May 03

sit this one out

all around me
there are parties
celebrations
laughter
   (real or feigned)
and I am
here
trying to figure out
how to make it
through
tomorrow

August 03

the game

solitaire
is consolation
in an
isolated world
distraction
from loneliness
occupation for
my rusty
blackened
mind

sometimes I win

August 03

diversions

I live in fantasies
now
movies
tv

with little life of my own
I live others'
thankful they are there
for salvation

the highpoint
of my day
around five
is playing solitaire
   drinking a martini
   watching your picture

August 04

accumulation

a huge snowball
rolling slowly
relentlessly
downhill
begun as a first-sized
iceball
meant for one of life's
    hard knocks
as it rolled
slowly downhill
it gathered detritus
in its path
a dead car battery
a broken water heater
two beautiful
large
sleek dogs
in the prime of
    their lives
struck down by
accident and
a merciful murder

it rolls
quietly
undeterred
headed for a
vulnerable being
her shoulder weakened by
sudden
longlasting
grief
it engulfs and crushes
her
and lazily slows to a satisfied
stop
its work accomplished

February 04

crack

yesterday
the car cracked
refused to go
its synapses damaged
then the garage door
refused to lower
stopping midway
as if it thought it was
hitting something
  or someone

the piece of burnt toast
inside me
cracked
unmendable
the crumbs scattering

soon
a global crisis
       a comic-book
       zigzag
       crack
will start
at the arctic circle
and create
a deep
complete
unmendable
abyss
rending the world
in pieces

February 04

new vista

in past
turning points
    a mating
    a birth
I chose not
to reflect
on the new life I
faced
simply slipped
seamlessly
into it

now I hesitate
frozen in the shadow
gazing suspiciously
at the bright
horizon
no mate or
baby
in the picture
to ease my move
forward

May 04

One of the strategies I used to cope with depression was to organize—the house, my thoughts, my hopes.

> February 04
> GOALS
> I. Reduce depression – how?
>   A. Being with people regularly
>   B. Being busy at home – house chores, transcripts, needlework
>   C. Walking 1/day with dog (ask someone to join)
>   D. Getting enough rest
>   i. 1 full pill/night. Don't try to reduce now. You need a full night's sleep
>   ii. nap/lie-down – arrange the day for it
>   E. Eating well
>   F. Being active/productive/helping (several friends could use a call)
>   G. Solitaire, crosswords
> II. Back pain – exercise, stress reduction, rest, physical therapy

This goal outline seems absurd now, but at that time I was doing a lot of fantastic thinking/hoping/planning, and just getting such an outline on paper cajoled me into thinking that I might have accomplished something.

* * *

When my friend Barbara Killinger lost her husband two months after Art died, I wrote her, hoping to help.

> *Dear Barbara,*
> *I cannot get it together to cook a lovely meal (as you would) and bring it to you, but my gift instead is this list of observations I've made on my own grieving. You can toss it all out, or you may find one or two things that resonate with you. I hope they help a little.*
> *Grief is physical pain. I have a rectangle of iron pressing on my chest most of the time. I am pretty much bereft of resources to solve problems – big or little, deal with*

frustrations, be disagreed with, add two and two, remember to do things. The least little negative thing seems over-whelming. I write everything down on the calendar—and try to remember to look at it.

My short-term memory has disappeared. It wasn't very good to begin with (aging) but now the problem is much greater.

My energy level is very low. I found that early morning is the only time I can work on anything that takes much energy, and as the day proceeds, my energy fades. I try to take naps, but then I forget to do so. But I think my energy level directly affects grieving, so I try to get plenty of rest before I have to tackle anything that requires energy (like the unavoidable income taxes).

I've found that movies and TV help to distract me now. At first, only crossword puzzles distracted – they don't have hospital scenes, or death scenes, or love scenes.

At least I'm eating well and sleeping relatively well. At first I resisted taking the tranquilizer I told you about, but then for a while I was taking one every night. Right now, I don't need it much, but I can't count on any condition lasting very long. The grief changes somewhat every day, so I haven't the foggiest notion how I'll feel tomorrow or next week. So I don't plan much ahead at all, and let my friends know that. They accept it well.

I try not to let others make any demands on me – such as some of my activist friends. This may be hard for you, as it has been somewhat for me, because you're not used to it—but you can do it if you keep in mind that you must be kind to yourself above all others right now. I told one that I thought I could do a rather complex task on the computer but had to call her later, after I tried, and tell her I simply wasn't up to it, and she understood.

My family has been enormously supportive and comforting. If I could have written a blueprint for each of them, they wouldn't have turned out any differently. There is an even greater bond among us now because we share grieving, and there is so much comfort in talking with them, because we can be completely ourselves together. hat's a wonderful mutual comfort.

I called in my chits – and found that some of the kindnesses I've shown to others have come back a hundredfold. That should work well for you, since you've shown so much kindness and hospitality to so many people over the years.

One thing I'm certain of: friends want to help. And everyone who does finds their own particular, personal way of doing it. Each time I've asked something of someone they acted as if I was doing them a favor to let them help me. One of the first things we learned in graduate school was that it's a lot easier to help than be helped. So I do my friends a favor by letting them do things for me. I found that some people will figure out what needs to be done and do it; others need to be asked. Both kinds of people have provided comfort for me.

Once, after a day of terror, I made a list of people I could call whenever I needed help, and set copies near each phone. Sometimes I'm so far down that I have trouble picking up the phone to ask, but I've been able to wait it out until I can.

I've tried to avoid other losses of any kind—for instance, I get rid of fading flowers or dying plants immediately.

Lots of times I'm functioning relatively well: keeping up with the level of orderliness that I need, feeding the dog, fish and birds, and doing whatever else I need to do. Then something comes in from left field and I'm down. Right now, and it's six weeks since my Art died (I hate that word), I'm functioning much more than not. I do, however, make sure that I tell friends, when they ask how I am and seem really to want to know beyond the "okay" that I give them, just how I'm feeling at that moment. I think it helps them to be able to talk about it, and about their own grief. We all miss him. I try to remember to ask, "How are you doing?" but I don't always make it. Grief, I've found, has made me terribly self-absorbed, and that's okay. I know it goes with the territory, and friends do, too.

As I said, these are only the things that I've seen in myself, and some of the remedies that seem to work for me right now. You'll find your own way. The only prescription I really want to give you is to be kind to yourself.

I love you.

April 27, 2003

I've figured out that for me there are four faces of grief (right now).

– an infinite, aching, horrible sadness of missing him. It comes most of the time in the bedroom where I see his clothes or just feel the intimacy of the bedroom—and mostly at night, when my energy level is at its lowest, and I'm really alone. It's good to have the dog there with me then. But the sadness is unbearable. I ache to hold him, to laugh with him, to talk with him, to just feel him around me as I used to, knowing that he's behind my back, or downstairs, or coming home soon, or waiting for me at home. The sadness is the most painful. I find no help in memories of him—they are not sweet, but painful.

– depression. The feeling that it will never get any better, that the world is a dark, black, unfriendly place where there is no future for me, and for the past few months, no past. I wonder how long? how long? I get out of bed in the morning and put one foot in front of the other, as everyone says, but it's just that. I have to push myself to do almost everything and take little pleasure in anything. Diversion, as Jim Edwards keeps saying, helps. I can temporarily forget, if I'm with others.

– anxiety. When I drive, I worry about causing accidents or killing people. Sometimes I hyperventilate, or lose track of what I'm doing. I forget. My short-term memory is shot. When Barca died, I was so out of it that I had no memory, a few days later, of having made several calls to people to tell them that I had lost my precious dog. When things get really bad, I make them worse by conjuring up the two most horrible, most unbearable images of my memory: of seeing Barca in the car, foaming at the mouth, falling down between the front and back seats, and dying. And worst of all, seeing Art's heart on the outside of his body as he lay dying. Reliving that terrible nightmare of a week end. How horrible it was, and is, to recall. And yet I joked—when Amy asked me what the heart looked like, I drew a valentine and said that his heart had "SA and AA" written across it. I was living in a fog then, moving through it ithout understanding any of the reality—or very little of it.

– other people. I have to create my relationships all over again. For close friends, there is a continuity. For my larger circle, I have to explain how I'm feeling—"It's rough – or better, it's tough—but I'm making it all right today." Those are the words my therapist and I developed to get the message through that I'm not all right, or "fine" but at least I can leave others with something to say, not uncomfortably tongue-tied.

Being in a group with some people who don't know what I'm going through—laughing, listening, cracking wise—is very hard on me and takes its toll. I come home exhausted and fearful and teary. I long to—but can't—turn to someone at the table and say, "I'm hurting terribly, you know. Please help me get through this." So I have to get used to the extreme discomfort of pretending to be other than what I am, of being inauthentic—almost intolerable for me—and realize that a subsequent meltdown will be the price. Otherwise, I never go out, and I see only 5 or 6 people. Not healthy.

How long? Only murky nothingness lies ahead and all around me. I can't do this yet I must. I hate it. Hate it. Hate it.

I remember a tale told in a movie (I can't remember the name of it), by the characters who spoke of a custom practiced by a tribe in Africa. If a family member was killed by another member of the tribe, the grieving survivors were helped through their grief by this custom: members of the tribe set the murderer adrift on the sea, leaving him to die, while the grieving family looked on. If they did not choose to rescue the perpetrator, they would continue to mourn their loss forever. Caring for another thus becomes an essential part of moving out of the worst part of grief. This made ultimate sense to me.

first dinner party

opening a package of
frozen food for
one friend
pleased to be
doing something
for someone else
having someone
in the house

October 03

Eventually I noticed a small change.

May 19 2004

As I was gardening yesterday at 6 pm, I suddenly realized that I was tired, but not too tired to decide, after a day of chores and errands and a lovely lunch with Sheryl Weir, that there was still time for me to get some needed gardening done.

Only a few months ago, I had to tell people, by way of explanation, that I had energy only in the morning hours. Around 1 o'clock I would lie down for a nap and then spend the rest of the day in low-energy pursuits, which I don't even remember now. But yesterday when I looked back on a full day, and didn't even get around to making my martini until 7 pm, I was gratified to see that a lot of my energy has come back. This may be due to not having back pain, and, in the past few days, not even having neck pain. Energy levels have been my best indicator of the progress I'm making in this long journey toward wholeness.

I also decided a couple of weeks ago that I was going to stay around the house this summer, using my time to get the attic, garage and basement cleaned out. Pulling out his clothes in the various closets and drawers in the house and giving them away will add to the closure. Maybe then will I be able to plunge back into my earlier activities, and even do some traveling.

I'm at a unique crossroads here: I can shape my life into anything I want to do, and I have the ability and the money to plan out my life exactly how I want it to be—something like a combination of personal fulfillment and service. And I've got a lot of talents to give, to both others and myself. It's a good place to be, but I'd exchange it all to have him back.

In the summer of the second year, with some of my newfound energy and help from friends, I cleaned the basement, attic and garage, and used some of my savings to put in a much-needed new driveway and sprinkler system. These projects were partly for my personal safety and ease of maintenance and partly for control. I wanted desperately to stay in this big old house, and I knew what a burden it could be for me to maintain it. Besides, tasks, I quickly discovered, took my mind off my grief.

Even as I worked on strengthening my muscles so I could carry and fix things for myself, I was still very glad to use the willing labor of young

Justin from across the street, and my longtime contractor John. They were both willing to take on the tasks I couldn't do, either for pay or for a glass of wine. And two years later Mikhail, a Russian chemist in his 40s doing research and teaching at University of Detroit Mercy, came to live here.

He was a gem, who seemed to need to do things for me, and he really enjoyed solving problems, like my sick vacuum cleaner, my VCR, a couple of door locks, and countless other household repairs. He gradually became a friend, and I missed him mightily when he went home to his family in Moscow.

This poem, written several years earlier, is still pertinent. I was to experience this phenomenon to a much deeper degree after I lost Art. Even three years later, I found myself digging my fingernails into a couch in agony when I watched a movie depicting the loss of a beloved. It brought everything back like a lightning bolt. Then, however, after a moment to catch my breath, I was able to recoup and go on. I know this will happen over and over, and each time it does I may find more strength to deal with it.

Art's colleague and our dear friend Dave Wineman was a special person in our lives. I once asked Art if he minded if I was in love with Dave. "Not at all," he replied. "I'm in love with him too." His death was a deep loss for us, and that loss would revisit me each time I heard of another friend's death.

echo

old grief - considered
controlled now -
   over time and distance
will crop up with sudden
ferocity
and overwhelm, overcome
the way yesterday fogs
dim and
unrecoverable
while childhood memories
stand still clear, shining,
detailed

another's sorrow, her
headback wail,
breaks the cocoon in which
mine has
been languishing.

1996

Dear Suzanne -

I'm sure you've received notes such as this by the trunkload over the last few weeks, but permit me to express how deeply, deeply saddened I was over Art's death. From the time I met him the very first time I dined at your home in 1977, I came away impressed by his extraordinary graciousness, wit, and sincere desire to make one feel truly welcome. On the numerous occasions over the intervening years when the two of you opened your doors to the Nichols family - the available slots in your spare bedrooms were vied over and I, being unabashedly spoiled, elbowed my way to the front of the line with not the slightest vestige of shame - the opportunity to enjoy the hospitality which you both so unselfishly extended was like being handed a free pass to the best B&B in town. He was truly the sort of bon vivant ("entertaining" is the word that keeps appearing to me, high praise indeed in my mind) that made my visits to Detroit much anticipated and memorable.

It was also so obvious to me that he loved you profoundly. I shall miss him. -

William Nichols
Ellen Parrish's brother

support

bed and bereavement

the women come
gradually forming themselves
   into a pattern
   of visitation
each now has her own bed
linens
and napkin ring

they get away from
their cares and sorrows
to mine

April 03

support

the dynamics of friendship
have shifted
some hold steady
(I knew they would)
some rise like goddesses
   out of the sea
unexpectedly close
warm and dependable
and lasting

some fade
(they don't know how to
say it
so they don't)

June 03

janice

I open the door
and fresh
fresh air comes in
shooting out bursts
of life and
ideas

gentle suggestions
exchanging
my suffocating
atmosphere
without
tainting
hers

Jan 04

I consider myself a wealthy woman in friends and family. I know that my healing came from many places: the beautiful 30 years I had with him, the healthy mind and body I had, an essential ethos of optimism and life. But I could have never made it without my friends and family. I depended on them as never before in my life, and discovered just how important they were and are to my wellbeing.

Pao Yu called often, and often showed up at my door with her still-warm freshly-baked bread under her arm, coming in for a talk. Sometimes she would tell my other friends when I was in bad shape, and they would call me. Janie opened the door for me when I sped to her house in tears, and held me while I cried. She came with me to take Art's ashes to the cemetery, and she came with me to put the dog down, weeping with me on both occasions. Each week for several weeks, Janice wrote me a supportive, thoughtful note, sometimes enclosing a poem that I came to treasure. She was the first of the women to come regularly to spend the night, telling me that being in my house was good for her. Kathleen came, looking at all the utensils in Art's kitchen and weeping—then sharing a martini with me and sitting down to a delicious meal that she cooked, sometimes from my meager stores. My son Jim, hearing of the generosity and overnight visits of these women, later sent us out for a "gift dinner" for all of us to enjoy—a lovely celebration of friendship.

When I woke up early and found myself alone for the first time, I reached for the phone to call Pat, who had lost her husband several years before. (Another of the ones who said, "Call me anytime, day or night.") "How do you get up out of bed?" I asked. Without hesitation (she must have done this before) she answered, "Turn on the radio. It will let the world in, a little at a time." I discovered then that something I had taken for granted all my life—just getting up in the morning—would have to be learned all over again.

Many other friends called and came to see me often. Helen Samberg urged me to call at any time of the day or night, "even if it's only to cry"—which I often did. She talked me, coaxed me out of several dark moods. Stan and Barbara Bernstein called often from Yellow Springs, hosted my Gentile shiva, came often to visit, invited me there, listened sympathetically over numerous phone calls, and held me when I broke down. Neighbors Frank and Keith came to stack my firewood and help with the fish tank. Frank had lost his wife several years before. "I know how it is," he said, and I knew he knew. Some months later, Anita came, over several days, and helped me clean my attic and basement, telling me she really enjoyed the feeling of organization it gave her.

> July 15, 03
>
> Helen keeps telling me not to be so hard on myself. I really didn't know what she meant, but Corinne tells me that I'm unrealistic in expecting energy when grief has robbed me of most of it. Helen keeps saying, "Look, it's only been...months!" That is comforting to hear that—and six months as opposed to 32 years is hardly enough time to adjust to a completely new life that I'm trying to build for myself after the roof caved in and left me in the basement covered with rubble.

(There were, of course, those who didn't seem to know anything about my needs, or about interacting with a grieving person. To my shock, they seemed able to ignore my situation and go on cheerily with their lives. Or worse, criticize me for something I was doing at the time. Armed with no defenses, I simply withdrew from their presence and collapsed, completely defeated and depressed. Corinne and my friend Barbara Bernstein helpfully labeled such people as "toxic" to me, and I was more than relieved to take their suggestion not to see any of them for a while. None of them was a really good friend, so it was not much of a loss. I rekindled an acquaintance with them later, as I regained my energy.)

I cried. A lot. Alone, or in the middle of a sentence when I was talking to others and couldn't hold it in. Expressing my emotions has always come naturally to me, and I know that doesn't hold true for all of us. But I am quite sure that holding in grief, trying not to cry, putting on a brave face or a stiff upper lip never really helps. Crying—and even screaming or wailing when I was alone—released the tension. And when I talked to friends and would begin at some point to cry, I was, without knowing it, creating a situation that made it more natural for me to ask for help when I needed it, and for them to give it.

Much of this is cultural, of course. People from some cultures value the "stiff upper lip" tradition, seeing the exhibition of any emotion as taboo and embarrassing. Other cultures expect grief to be expressed, with sound and fury.

Like many people, I found it hard to ask for help. I fell back on what I had learned in my first year at the School of Social Work. In one class, the professor divided the group in two and assigned each roles: one asking for help, the other responding with it. Then we exchanged sides. With that exercise we all became convinced of how helping is far easier than asking for help.

Although I consider myself generally mentally healthy and self-confident, asking for help doesn't come naturally to me. I tend to value my independence and have always preferred to live by the I-can-do-it-myself-thank-you way of life. One time when Art and I were canoeing in Canada with our friends the Bernsteins, I found myself sitting on the shore, physically exhausted by a particularly strenuous day. Art was busy pitching the tent, and I really needed some help with some equipment. As I sat there staring at the damned stuff and utterly unable to lift it, Stanley Bernstein came over to me. Sizing up the situation and never one to mince words, he said, "You have trouble asking for help, don't you, Suzanne?" I couldn't argue with him. I certainly did.

But in 2003, in the dark, dark days, I learned. I learned because I was desperate, and eventually got so good at it that I lost my shyness about asking. And I always found that friends were more than willing to do things for me. Eventually I came to apply one criterion when asking a favor: Would I do this for him/her? Then s/he will be willing to do it for me. That made it easier for me to ask.

Years before Art died, I learned from a widow how supportive it is when someone else shares their grief and sense of loss with you. "I miss him, too" were words of great comfort to her. So I was always attentive whenever anyone would mention him—their memories of him, or who he was.

August 15 '03
Cape Cod

Stanley, drawing me aside from the dinner table, where I've set a wine glass for Art: "This is not in my set of beliefs, but sometimes I feel his presence around me. Do you feel like that?":

"I still write him letters."

"Okay," he turns and announces to everyone. "I'm going to sit next to Art. And so is Suzanne."

Peter asks me what my day is like, and it's a great opportunity to let them see what I'm going through. Lynn comes over to our cottage, without Arwen, for a quiet time to talk—just talk.

> *I am pleased. I am also pleased to discover that Arwen's middle name, Alythia, is also part of the tribute to Thor—with both of her names beginning with As, as his did.*
>
> *Anne tells me that Stanley tells her that he misses Art— and Art-and-Suzanne. That makes me very sad, and I know I am not back yet.*

There are two sides to everything, of course, and that includes support. In my depression I had periods of feeling terribly sorry for myself, and sometimes that turned into anger at imagined slights.

bitter mood

having loved the man
does not condemn you to
support the widow
in loneliness

anger
resentment
zing in
and zoom out at
those who do not call
who go about their busy
lives
and do not call
do not think of sharing a
meal with me
in my loneliness
depression
desperation

I hate

October '03

...but some of my friendships turned sour. On the Monday following Art's memorial, my friend Joan, having flown in from the west coast, came to stay with me. As she was leaving on Wednesday afternoon, I began to fall apart. I cried and begged her not to go. "I can't," she answered tersely. It shocked me, but I told her I understood and I said good bye. What could be more important, I asked myself later, than a good friend begging you to stay with her? It took me months to realize that she was saying that she simply couldn't take any more of my grieving. Even after I understood, I couldn't forget that awful moment. Months later, I visited her in her home state, and the visit went very badly, for a number of reasons not directly related to this incident. I no longer see her. She had been a close friend for over 45 years.

I kept an "emergency" list below the phone in my kitchen with names and phone numbers of people I could call for anything (of course I always had my daughter and son, whom I called often): to listen while I vented and cried and ranted and vented some more; to come and stay all night with me; to go to lunch or dinner (mealtimes were some of the worst); to come over and help me read instructions so I could do such simple things as changing the fish tank filter (I couldn't concentrate on any kind of reading for more than a paragraph without becoming hopelessly confused—I cancelled the newspaper and didn't read anything for many months).

And they came. They came willingly without ever making me feel they were inconvenienced. They came gladly as if they were waiting to be asked. They came eagerly as if they enjoyed the task and even enjoyed being with me (I thought I was terrible company, for the most part, but I always brightened whenever I had friends around).

Much later, one of my friends told me that she learned how to ask for help from me. I took this as a great compliment, especially since it had taken me so long to learn it for myself. I came to see this valuable life skill as a part of the Great Education of Grief.

good intentions

I'm getting tired
of working to
understand
my friends
who have had
to go on
their lives
while I am stuck
here in mine
frozen
and lonely

please
please
do not make me
listen to
how often
you think
of me
and make the decision
not to call

December 03

drugs

getaways

the first sip of coffee
the first slug of martini
are the best tastes of
the day

both drugs

August 03

time extension I

I wish martinis
lasted a little longer so
I could sip one for
an hour or so

they disappear
so quickly
mine lasts only
a few minutes
and the cheese
is still there

July 03

February 28

I am afraid of having to take pills each night for sleep. It's 1:30; I couldn't nap this afternoon and I finally gave in. "That's what they're there for," I hear Corinne say. But I'm afraid. When does it end? How will I know when I can sleep again without them? Crossword puzzles are better than reading or TV: in crosswords, there is no sadness, no death, no hospital scenes, no reminders. Tomorrow I talk to Corinne.

There is so much talk of addiction in our society and so little of pain relief. Although the pharmaceutical companies are on their way to make us all dependent on their products, people who have real addictive tendencies are certainly a minority. But for too long doctors have been more concerned with this minority than with the majority of their patients who are in real pain. While most of us are still haunted by unnecessary guilt and fear when we take medication for legitimate pain, these attitudes are slowly changing (my son has always been on the good side of this issue). Such was the case when my doctor, a good one, gave me sleeping pills, at my request. They provided me with relief and respite from the day-to-day fears and depression I needed to escape from. I ended up taking them for over a year, constantly having to defend myself to myself about dependency, yet knowing I couldn't face nights without sleep. I weaned myself off them in April of 2004, when I really knew I was ready to sleep without them.

writing

I wrote journals to calm down, to try to clarify what was happening to me, to clarify my feelings about it all.

I didn't think about it; writing was just one of the several means to sanity. In my worst, most depressive moments, I could call someone to talk and cry with, or I could write. Each action served in a different way to calm me, and there was no rhyme or reason for choosing one over the other. But writing had one advantage over talking: I was aware enough to be careful to date my writing, so desperate was I for some sign of progress, some sign that I had moved from the cold dead center toward some kind of normality, calmness. And in my desperation I knew that reading these journals and poetry at some future date would prove to me that I had indeed moved. Part of me really didn't believe that I would ever feel normal again.

Some of the journals were a kind of stream of consciousness; others were set down as a record. But the poetry was quite different. Some of the poems ("milestone" "the closet" in Things; "perspective" and "watching" in Loneliness) were written simply as self-observations, hoping to begin the problem-solving process by becoming aware of what I was feeling.

In others I used metaphors ("maelstrom" in Loneliness; "holidays" in Holidays) to remove the dense feelings to another sphere, where they were clarified and gave me in no small measure a kind of control over them. I felt somehow better when I finished a poem, almost as if I had captured the current sorrow and transformed it into something I could deal with, something a little remote from myself, and therefore less painful.

respect

I have mentioned several times the importance of seeing grief as a unique experience (see also "Drugs"). Some grieve loud and long, and some of this is perfectly acceptable in certain cultures. Some people seem not to grieve at all. Some of us talk at length about it; others cannot talk about it at all. And some of those experience a delayed grief, one that surfaces months later in the most unlikely situations that seem to have nothing to do with the loss. I think that holding in—repressing—strong emotions like grief very often takes its toll. But however one expresses— or doesn't express—one's grief deserves to be respected and accepted.

I needed this perspective from my friends when my grieving went on for over a year and a half. It turned out that they were more understanding of me than I was.

> March 11/ 04
> *...some of this, I'm sure, comes from my feelings of boredom, frustration, wanting (perhaps) to get back into the world a little and yet being afraid to do so. But I'm feeling that some people in the world outside are saying "enough" to me. (And I realize that this is a lot of projection on my part—). Words like "wallow" and "lighten up" and get on with your life" and "why do you still…" and "you're making it difficult for the rest of us to be sympathetic" are swirling around in my consciousness. Are people actually saying these words, or do I imagine them?*
>
> *Well, I've heard a few of those words, so I'm not imagining all of it. And I'm working on myself, what I want to do, what I want to be doing soon. I've just done a major thing: I emailed David [Barsamian, whose Alternative Radio I had worked for] and told him I wanted to start writing transcripts for him again. I can do them now, my back pain allowing, half an hour at a time. That eases me back into actually taking part in other activities again. When, I don't know, but I'm not locking*

myself into a date. At least I'm now thinking about doing it, where I couldn't even consider it a month ago.

Another thing: friends now say, "Okay, you're better." I know that I've caused them a lot of pain, because they feel so sorry for me. I know that. And now, they think, "she's better" so they can relax a little. But as soon as I hear that I think: now they're going to desert me. Now they're going to assume I am like everybody else in the world, and I don't need help. But I do need help, and support, and calls, and dinners and all the rest of the care that I've had. I do need it. And it scares me that people are going to drift away.

Many times I wanted to cry out, "I'm me! I can't help being me, and I want to be accepted as me, my grief accepted as okay. And of course it was by my friends. "It takes as long as it takes," Kathy Rashid blessedly observed.

I learned, out of that experience, that it is essential for all of us to accept the grieving of others, no matter how weird or asocial or extraordinary—or even what we normally accept. For that reason, I have included the grieving experiences of several people. Each one is unique, as are human beings, and each one expresses the real and miserable sadness of loss.

THE EXPERIENCES
OF OTHERS

Ellie Tudor

(Steve Tudor's sailboat was found on Lake St. Clair in 1994. His body was never recovered.)

For some reason, I really wanted to talk about it, so I did some journaling on the subject. And from this view—10 years later—what I did was pretty pragmatic, I think. I have never thought of myself as particularly strong and resilient. I felt so weak—and I had to keep lying down—and I didn't know what I wanted really—in the face of the loss. But, for some reason I had some really strong feelings about what I "didn't" want—and most of them I realize now had to do with avoiding pain. I have never liked to suffer. And I see now how these very practical things saved me.

1) I didn't want people to be sad when they were around me—so I did everything I could to cheer them up—and to be silly.

2) The pain was pulling me under and I didn't want to be pulled into a depression and have to take drugs. I am very opposed to taking drugs. So I told myself whatever I needed to—to keep from feeling the pain (i.e., He's not gone. We'll see each other soon.). Basically, I did whatever I had to to find peace—even if I had to lie to myself. Basically, I tried to find thoughts that gave me peace—whether they were true or not. I've always said, "I'm Cleopatra Queen of de Nile." I think denial has gotten a bad rap.

3) I allowed myself to grieve and feel the loss and fall on the floor and sob when I was alone.

4) I drank beer and wine and manhattans.

5) Thinking of the future stretching on and on without Steve was unthinkable—so I took one day at a time—and one moment at a time.

6) I didn't want our connection to be broken. (Michael told me immediately "We are all connected." and this was so comforting to me that I clung to it like a liferaft.) So, I talked to Steve. I apologized to him for things and told him how I loved him. I saw him helping me with whatever I needed help on. I saw him watching over me and taking care of me. I talked to him about all the wonderful things that we had done together—and what were my favorites and why, etc. etc. I reminded him of life-changing things that he had said to me.

7) I didn't want Steve's death to overwhelm his life for me—as had happened with the loss of my parents. So again, a celebration of the life and a present on-going connection were very important.

Anyway, thanks for asking. Sorry to go on and on, but it's very nice to be able to share these things with someone who understands. I tried to write poetry, but I don't have the gift. It is a very wonderful thing to be able to write poignantly and with immediacy about what you are going through, which is very healing for you—as well as for others who can see themselves through you. As my son Michael says so eloquently: "We are all connected." So, as we heal ourselves, we also help to heal others.

Lavanya Krishnan

(Her grandmother died when Lavanya was 18. She wrote this ten years later.)

I can still smell the freshly ground pepper, the scent of fresh green coriander waiting to be pounded into chutney…my favorite kind…the sweet fragrance of lilies that wafted in the cool summer breeze…for it was summer. Not the hot, scotching usual Indian summer but a glowing little summer with just enough warmth to remind you of the time of the year, but not enough to taunt you into stop loving it.

I can still smell the sweet scent of ripe mangoes mingled with the sour tingling scent of tamarind. I can still hear the monotonous grinding sound as continuous as the hum of bees with momentary halts like gentle breaks between a zooming ride.

I can still smell the rain as my thick hair was combed by two gentle hands. I can still feel the loving touch as oil…coconut oil was rubbed into them.

I can still hear the gentle rebukes when I had gorged myself on chocolates. I can still feel the texture of her sarees when I had buried my face in them. I can still smell the sweet scent of powder…the kind she always used…the kind I loved to smell.

I can still feel the stinging tears that stained my face one day. Now the sting has gone…and so have the tears. All that remains is a memory, a beautiful memory – My Grandmother.

Leslie Zillman

(Leslie's partner Marilyn died of undiagnosed cancer after they were together for four years.)

The hospital parking lot was flanked by tall, old straight pine trees that looked like silent soldiers guarding all that was inside. Snow was falling out of the quiet sky…featherlike, about the size of a quarter. Each flake fell about a foot away from the other before they reached the ground. We had just disconnected life support, and like a car that runs out of gas you came to a stop and were gone. I was stunned. It was hard to stay in the here and now. I wanted to be one of those snow flakes and just ride the silence.

I tried to remember what I was doing and where I was going...should I be doing something? Should I be going some where? Are there more people to be notified? Jean, your twin sister said she was surprised you went so went so fast. People with such damage don't usually linger, but I couldn't say this to her.

All the years I worked as a hospital social worker had been in my face all that week watching you spiral out of control, slipping away. I knew early in the crisis that you didn't have much of a chance. I know too much. I know how babies die. They breathe their last tiny breath with the confidence they will breathe another. But you knew you were going to die for a year or more even though the cancer diagnosis came just ten days ago. It was massive, in every major organ system and of unknown origin. I saw death in your eyes early that year. Death by doctors not looking, not caring to look beyond a depressed middle aged woman, for anything more that might kill her sooner than a depression. Death by a family believing, as always, that you were malingering, expecting you to pull yourself up by your bootstraps and stop whining. Death by me your wimp-partner who couldn't get you to take charge of your health and deal with it. You started dying long before the ventilator was turned off—or maybe you always knew and chose death over the horrifying cancer torture they call treatment.

At that moment I just needed to find my car and see if I could remember where to put the key in the door and get in and drive myself home before I drifted away from the snowy silent afternoon.

We had hardly left the hospital in the last ten days. Especially me; I was afraid I couldn't get back in. I had lied to get into ICU. They asked me if I was family and I said I was her sister. I didn't know what this hospital's rules were about Lesbian couples. Barb, Marilyn's first partner of 12 years (and still good friend) said she was Marilyn's sister too...for the same reason. Marilyn's sister Jean was kind enough to go along with the lie. This was all hard enough and she knew we needed to be there with Marilyn. I knew I could have spent the whole crisis sitting alone in the hospital lobby. Over the years Marilyn and I had seen other Lesbian couples separated from each other at a partner's death bed because of hospital rules.

I knew she was dying and I wanted to be there with her. Flashes of rage would come over me just thinking about the possibility of being taken away from her death bed. There was so much muddy water about this death anyway and that worry just added more for all of us trying to help, regardless of our relationships. It was on everyone's mind; people caring for Marilyn could see weren't sisters.

I felt powerless. Things hadn't been good between us for some months, like a lot of Marilyn's relationships. I was exhausted all the time, stretched financially and always worried about losing my job from taking off so much time to take care of her and me. Family leave policies don't apply to Lesbian partners, who aren't recognized as spouses in employment benefit programs. Often I took time off as leave without pay or an unexcused absence.

Up until the last ten days of her life she had been badly treated by the medical community and in these last weeks she wanted nothing to do with doctors. They hadn't listened to me either. We were low priority, middle aged women with concerns for her health and the care she wasn't getting. Middle aged women are a low priority in health care, and our being Lesbian didn't improve our status.

Medical people can be led by their own biases. Over and over again they refused to look beyond her depression for a diagnosis. She talked about pain in her lower abdomen and cramps in her legs. They looked at her as much as to say she was crazy and ordered only the bare minimum of physical tests. The coroner's preliminary ruling on cause of death was "suspicious." He was appalled, finding nine sites of cancer in the body and no cancer diagnosis prior to her admission to the hospital ten days before her death. Months later, the medical examiner ruled the origin of the cancer as uterine. She had to die to get a true diagnosis beyond depression.

Jean was desperate to understand what killed her. She was able, as I was not, to get Marilyn's medical records and talk with the doctors who had seen her in those last three years, trying to fit the pieces together. I still think mostly what Marilyn died from is the job this country has done in taking the care out of health care. When people asked me how I was feeling I couldn't tell them. How would they understand homicidal? I wanted to kill the health care system. The pressure on doctors, nurses and other workers to treat people faster and cheaper fragments care and sucks the humanity right out of the system.

For months I was dealing with a numbing sadness mixed with anger and disbelief that she had died at fifty—such a young age. I had lost my

Mother and three close friends in the few years before Marilyn's death. Grief felt like pounding waves in the storm: I couldn't get braced before the next one came. Grief on top of grief was nearly unbearable. Most of the time I had to force myself to pay attention to where I was and what I was supposed to be doing. I knew this vagueness was from grief. It was a veil shielding most of the sun and keeping joy at arm's length.

Support came from different places. The Lesbian community is a wonderful curse in life. It is like having a nation of big sisters who want to help and make sure you do things right so we all don't look bad. Tragedy is public, supported and shared in the community.

The community holds each individual to a high standard, probably because we have been kicked around more than the average bird. Everyone has a story. Situations for Lesbian women have improved over my lifetime, but there is still ample intolerance. We get thrown out of families, straight friend's lives, hospitals, good jobs, churches, housing, and the military... all because we love women instead of men. So we police our own and we learn from each other.

No matter how close they are to you, they want and expect details about a tragedy, particularly if it is losing a partner. They review it like a play-by-play and have an opinion about how they think it went and how you measured up. There is an urgency to talk with you, from their concern. Lesbians understand there are some people in your life who just won't understand the magnitude of your loss. But women in the Lesbian community are eager to show you their respect. There can be disagreements and sometimes people take sides. There is always some debate in the community about how things were handled. This might sound harsh, but it's really not. It is how we heal and get by the loss. When the community loses a friend and a couple, they need and want to debrief. Food comes too, anything from organic homemade to a bag of White Castles. We are a diverse bunch.

The best way we can deal with loss is to outlive the grief and take as good care of ourselves as we can. I knew that to survive this grief I needed to make some changes. I latched on to my writing. I found a wonderful teacher who taught me to use my writer's voice to express myself. Writing is empowering, a way to give to others and be witness to what is important in this world.

I learned to meditate from a Buddhist teacher. Through it and with her support I came out of the fog of grief and joy entered my life. Over time, Buddhism has become my spiritual home. I don't think I could have gotten where I am if I hadn't had writing and found a spiritual practice that works for me. These two wonderful teachers helped me grow as a writer and spiritual pilgrim. I would have died of a broken heart without them.

I am well beyond the fog of grief and the heartbreak of what Marilyn and I didn't get to do. She came into my life late in life and left almost as quickly as she came. We had four short years together, and much of that time she was ill.

Some things still catch me off guard. My voice cracks and tears may fall but mostly I remember the good stuff. The memory of her makes me smile. And the process goes on. I look forward to the future and treasure what I have gained from having her in my life. Joy rests peacefully in my heart.

Jackie Krueger

(Jackie and Doug were in their sixties with grown children and grandchildren, when Doug died suddenly, with no warning that he was ill.)

What hit me right away was how much I missed the level of joy I had with him—how lucky I was, and how now that joy was gone.

Doug left for a business week end. We had said our usual good-byes, looking forward to seeing each other when he returned. And then I got a phone call. Doug had dropped dead.

The shock was incredible. I had never felt that kind of shock, or that kind of deep depression before. He had left me alive, in good spirits, both of us looking forward to being together again, and he came back in a box. I did get some comfort from knowing that he had visited his brother in the town where he grew up while he was gone, and had also been with his best friend from high school. At least he was with loved ones. But he died of an apparent heart attack in the emergency room of the local hospital. I was heartbroken that I was not with him.

I'd never been really, really down in my life—those feelings were new to me, and I didn't know how to deal with them. I was never suicidal, but the deep depressions that lasted half an hour or more were shocking to me. I felt I truly understood what a broken heart was.

I tried to be brave, but the grief was like a Pandora's box. I held it in until someone would say something to me, or talk about grief, and then it would come tumbling out. During these times others would express their painful experiences associated with death and divorce, and it helped me to have that sharing time.

It took me six years to fully let go, and through those years I knew I needed a great deal of patience. I had to parcel out my grieving time.

I had to be careful about drinking. It would be so easy to pour a drink, take it back to the bedroom, and just continue...but I didn't. In the early days, the terrible days, what helped was to say to myself, "Just give me peace." The word itself, the sound of it, would calm me for a few hours, even on some rare days, for the whole day. Some friends urged me to travel, but I found travel—even to visit my daughter Carolyn—incredibly stressful. I think I was pushed into it before I was ready. It didn't "make everything better"—to the contrary, in some ways it made things worse. My friend and I went on a tour together, and I was not ready for how couple-oriented the tour was. I remember having strong feelings about being left out.

Doug had served in Viet Nam, flying helicopters—a highrisk assignment. He would be gone from us for a few weeks at a time, but he always managed to come back. (My daughter Sharon, six at the time, used to go into his closet and count how many clothes he had taken with him, to check out how honest he was being with her. I thought, after he died, how very grateful I was that he had not died on one of those missions, but instead had come back to us, so we were able to spend the next thirty years of our lives together. And we were close. He was always there with me, in the house, in the garden, making decisions, helping with chores, just being together.

So there were many little things in the house that reminded me of him—of us. We had spent some of the war years overseas, and brought back numerous keepsakes that brought back so many memories.

But of course there were frustrations. I wasn't ready to do the paperwork of loss, and there was so much of it—military and civilian. Although he and I made most financial decisions together, I wasn't used to doing the actual paperwork. After he died, I wanted to put it off, put off the finishing of it because that would make his death so terribly *final*.

And reading instructions for any household item was overwhelming. I needed some batteries, and once I got to the hardware store I realized that I didn't know what kind to buy—double A? Triple A?

I tried therapy for a while, but gave up on it. Group therapy, grief groups—didn't interest me, but I found a therapist who would see me alone. But I found myself annoyed at her telling me how well I was doing. I didn't feel I was doing well at all. Maybe I should have gone to someone else, but I just gave up on it. Another curious thing happened around the issue of the wedding band. A friend who lost her husband around the time that Doug died had taken off her wedding ring almost immediately (I don't think theirs had been a very close relationship), and kept asking me when I was going to do the same. I felt pushed in a direction I didn't want to go, and resisted the idea. A few months later, I found Doug's band, and slipped it on next to mine, where it looked just fine to me. I kept it on for several months and suddenly found that I couldn't separate the two bands. I wore them like that for a while until they separated on their own, and then I felt that it was time to take them off.

I'm not alone in the house Doug and I shared. My brother, who never married, came over one night to comfort me and spend the night, and then as a mutual decision, just moved in with me. He helps with my Mother who is in a nursing home, and I have someone to talk to—not a small essential. My neighbor offered, soon after Doug's death, to help with house and garden chores, and we agreed on recompense. Daughter Sharon lives close to me, and I talk to each of my daughters frequently. So I have come to terms with the tasks of everyday living. But nothing, no one, can replace him.

Mary Assel

(Mary Saad was 15 when she was married to a Muslim businessman and went with him to North Africa to live. It was an arranged marriage and during the first five years as she struggled to love him she bore him three children. For her, the relationship was one of submission to her husband's controlling ways. After ten years of marriage, Mary developed the self-esteem and determination to confront her husband. She threatened to leave him if he did not change. Faced with losing her, he learned to restrain his anger and relinquish some control to his wife.

As a result, they became closer, and 9 years later, when he fell ill with cancer, she loved and cared for him for a year until he died. Alone, she made arrangements after the burial and for the Isboua, the Muslim traditional sevenday period of visitation following a death. In less than a year, she arranged to close their business and prepare herself and her children for the move back to Dearborn, Michigan, her hometown.)

When Mahmoud died, I felt detached from the universe and more in touch with the mystical world of the dead. I could not associate with the living and found no reason to continue my own life even though my three teenagers were in desperate need of my support. My legs became weak and I began to limp from what the doctors labeled post-polio syndrome.

I was bedridden for two weeks. It wasn't until my son Mazen, begged me to help him with family matters that I forced myself to go to work and join a world that was foreign to me. It took at least a year for me to accept my husband's death or ironically my own fate and to continue life with the living. I wasn't able to genuinely reach out to my children for at least three years. I buried myself in my studies and in the search for a stable career. By then, my children began to search for a life of their own and five years after my husband's death, I began to date in order to fulfill the void that I was experiencing.

Mary remarried in at the age of 41, and another son was born. Three years later, her oldest son Mazen, then married, was diagnosed with an inoperable brain tumor. Despite one doctor's cruel prediction of death in two weeks, Mazen lived for an additional eighteen months, under the care of his mother, his wife Mona, and his sisters Rania and Dania.

When Mazen died, it was a déjà vu in terms of losing a loved one, but the intensity of my detachment from the world had quadrupled and to this date (5 years later) I do not feel that I will ever be the same and the only reason I am living is because I have no other choice. At first I continued to function as I did before because I had a three-year-old who indirectly reminded me that I could not collapse. I feared for his sanity because he was confused about death, angels and the afterlife. His constant cries and fear of death drew me back to this world only to set me on a different direction. In lieu of struggling with the unknown, I accepted what I did know (the notion that there was nothing I could do) so I searched for a path that might lead me to my son and that path was my religion: Islam.

My friends and family were present and readily available to assist me during both of my catastrophes, but they did not seem to connect with me nor I with them. I was very angry with the world and I took my anger out on everyone around me. I believe that the only time I felt good was when I detached myself from my surroundings and buried myself in religious books. It was my only solace.

My religion gave me the serenity I was searching for and it helped me through my grief more than anything. The intangibility of religion seemed to rhyme with obscurities behind my fear and hence directed me down a path that felt more soothing and peaceful than anything I'd ever experienced.

My culture gave me room to expand my grief in the sense that grieving for long periods of time is totally acceptable. It is not a taboo for Muslims to cry and wear black and I did so for over a year. Segregation from the living is tolerated, and not participating in the festivities of others is expected. Hence, my culture helped me contemplate creation and entrust my heart to God. It was the catalyst to my own understanding of God's intricate world and belief that He was holding my loved one in ultimate safety and care.

The loss of my husband turned me into a stronger and more affirmative parent. It also gave me the strength I needed to voice my opinion and the freedom to remove myself from the aura of co-dependency. The loss of my son made me more conscientious of a Superpower that I could not battle or confront, and I became more inclined to expect that a tragedy might happen during every waking moment of my life. I learned to become more sensitive to the needs of my other children and help them see that every sweet moment of our lives will never come again. Who knows when something might change our world and that I, or the recipients of my love and words of kindness, might be gone.

Marti Alston

(Marti's husband Chris was in a wheelchair for the duration of their marriage. Theirs was a racially mixed marriage and Chris was a good deal older than Marti. They were both active lefties in Detroit)

A friend asked me about the processes I went through after my husband Chris died. I had begun preparing for his death several years earlier. Being the kind of people who "Grab the mule by the tail and stare the facts in the face," we tried to prepare in advance for the time I would be alone. Chris pushed me to become as educated as I could. He saw that as a way of protecting me, helping to assure I would have decent employment. At the time he died, I had just begun a doctoral program. But I knew I would not finish it. I did it as my final gift to him. Chris and I wrote wills and made certain that his little pension had a survivor's clause in it. He spent virtually nothing on himself and insisted that I put any extra money into savings.

Beyond these practical considerations, we did not really talk about my life without him — that would have been too painful. But I thought about it privately, trying to imagine what it would be like.

After he died, I grieved — weeping whenever I drove by myself or for no apparent reason. And I went on what seemed like an endless roller coaster ride of emotional chaos, dropping into an abyss of depression or soaring to heights of euphoria. I would get very angry and would let people know it — something I had never done before. Okay, I admit it, I felt out of control.

I am convinced that what saved me was my determination to seek my own healthy way through the dark tunnel. And my confidence that such a path could be found. I began to really like the new, more expressive, me that emerged. I experimented with sculpting, watercolor painting, papermaking. The other saving grace was my decision to reach out to other women. My marriage had been a self-contained unit. We needed little else beyond our own company and multifarious activities. Reaching out to others took work and the confidence that people would respond to my outstretched hands. They did. I burrowed into the nurturing company of female friends.

Slowly, I seized control of my own life. I was able to do so because of the love I had shared with Chris. He had cared and supported me so much that I was confident that I could live on, and live in a meaningful way. I also felt that I brought him with me wherever I went. But this life was different from the one I had shared with Chris. At the end of 2 years, I knew it was time to physically move myself into a "Marti space" — one that I would define. In this new environment I read more, listened to music which was new to me, wrote poetry. Yet my surroundings still speak of my life with Chris — pieces from Africa, the Caribbean, Central America and the streets of Detroit. In short, I integrated the old and new me in a way that the re-invented Marti was a result of all her experiences — those with Chris and those after him. I felt comfortable with that.

None of these changes would have been possible just by force of personal will. Rather, they took place within the larger activist world which is central to my life. It fills me with optimism that the world is a place that can be changed, can be made more humane. It was the community of similarly committed individuals that helped see me through. I never felt alone or unloved.

Chris and I had fought together for justice and equality. It was a major part of our life together. It gave us purpose. It gave us joy. From the depths of the sorrow I felt when he died, from this journey I have described, I re-found that joy. I came to realize that meeting the needs of individuals and the society had to go hand in hand. Then, when you are in need, as I was, there exists a wonderful caring

conclusion

This book may not speak to everyone, but for those to whom it does speak, I am grateful to you for sharing these pages with me. The writing of it has served as a kind of catharsis, of closure and of some satisfaction from the positive feedback and shared observations that came my way when I sent sections to friends and friends of friends.

Grief, as I experienced it, has been life-changing for me. I am still grieving and will continue to be shot at, when I least expect it, by the in-my-face fact that my Art is never coming back. But my life is full, and so much of that fullness is a result of the life I had in the years we spent together.

I can only wish everyone a similar outcome.

Detroit
November 28, 2006